CHAPTER NEWS AND GENERAL
ACTIVITIES
LOS ANGELES
December 2, 1937

FORREST J ACKERMAN'S
W O R L D   O F
SCIENCE FICTION

At 9:30 P.M., after interesting period of informal discussion, meeting was called to order by Director Russ Hodgkins. Minutes of preceding meeting, including summary of lengthy debate, feature of the meeting, were read and approved.

Among the visitors were Neva Bradbury and friend, brought and introduced by member Ray Bradbury; Philip Fink, a fan recently from New York City; Leonard Adland; and Robert Lovelace. New member who supported our unofficial average of one per meeting was Wilbur F. Stimson.

At request of 4E Ackerman, a discussion was held regarding the future of the chapter organ, **Imagination!** He informed the club that more cooperative response to the enterprise was required to insure continued existence of the periodical, resulting in sufficient promises of service to enhearten somewhat those upon whose shoulders the work has been resting.

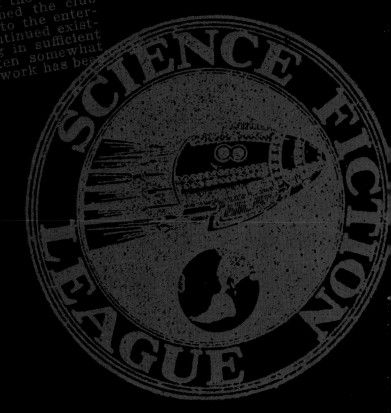

FORREST J ACKERMAN'S
W O R L D   O F
SCIENCE FICTION

Foreword by JOHN LANDIS   Preface by A. E. VAN VOGT

AURUM PRESS

Publisher: W. Quay Hays
Editorial Director: Peter Hoffman
Editor: Steven Baeck
Art Director: Kurt Wahlner
Production Director: Trudihope Schlomowitz
Color and Pre-Press Director: Bill Castillo
Production Artist: Gaston Moraga, Regina Troyer
Scanning Operators: David Chadderdon, Russell Lockwood
Production Assistants: Tom Archibeque, Gus Dawson
Copy Editor: Carolyn Wendt

First published in Great Britain 1998
by Aurum Press Limited, 25 Bedford Avenue, London WC1B 3AT

First published in 1997
by General Publishing Group, Inc., Los Angeles

A catalogue record for this
book is available from the British Library.

ISBN 1 85410 573 6

Printed in the USA
by RR Donnelley & Sons Company
10 9 8 7 6 5 4 3 2 1

General Publishing Group
Los Angeles

The art director and editor would like thank Dave Hunter, for generously
allowing access to his sci-fi books, souvenirs, and movie stills, which
complemented the author's remarkable collection.

Preceding pages: The citizens of *Metropolis* (1927) head off to work; the cast of *Flash Gordon* (1936); Dana Wynter and Kevin McCarthy flee from the pod people in *Invasion of the Body Snatchers* (1956) © Allied Artists; Bruce Willis in *12 Monkeys* (1995) © MCA/Universal; the *Enterprise* squares off against a Klingon destroyer in *Star Trek IV: The Voyage Home* (1986) © Paramount Productions; the stargate sequence from *2001: A Space Odyssey* (1968) © Metro-Goldwyn-Mayer; Yoda contemplates the future in *The Empire Strikes Back* (1980) © Lucasfilm LTD. **This and facing page:** 1930s rayguns inspired by *Buck Rogers* (1939). **Back cover images:** *The Day the Earth Stood Still* © 20th Century-Fox; *King Kong* © RKO Radio Pictures; *Independence Day* © 20th Century-Fox; *The X-Files* © 20th Century-Fox; *Star Trek* © Paramount Productions. **Back flap images:** *The Bride of Frankenstein* © Universal Pictures; Steven Spielberg and E.T. © Amblin Entertainment, Inc.

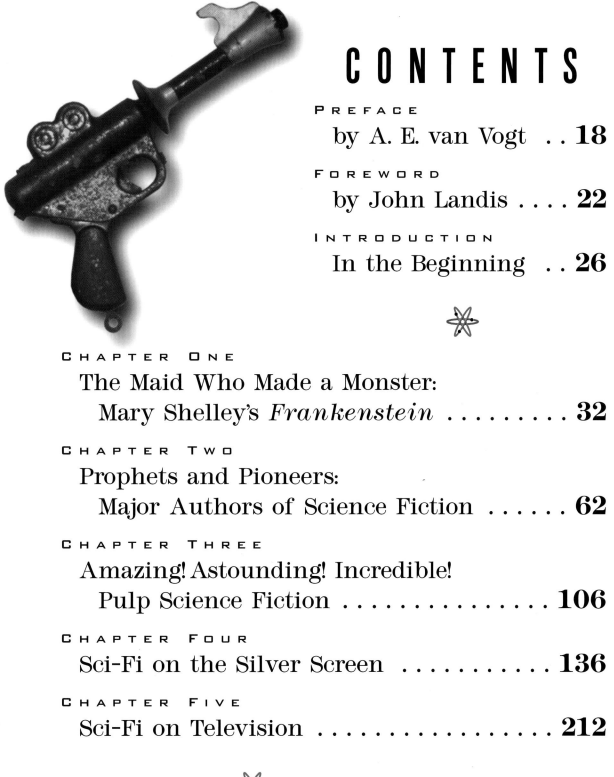

CONTENTS

How does one accurately describe the lifelong career of a man who has not only seen the birth and development of the movement we now call science fiction, but has participated from the beginning in a way that has had undeniable impact on the entire genre as we know it today? It takes a special kind of mind to accomplish this task, a mind that doesn't live within the same world or time as most of the rest of humanity.

This is Forrest J Ackerman. From the time he was born, he saw things that others didn't dare imagine: cities of the future, mental giants, robots, rockets to other planets and star systems, and extraterrestrial life-forms. Forry, as his friends call him, made contact with other great science fiction minds like his and formed newsletters, clubs, and conventions in order to share these special worlds with others. But why is Forrest J Ackerman's mind special in a modern world where science fiction is a mainstream pleasure? Simply because he was one of the founders who brought us to where we are today.

A. E. van Vogt. Photo by Jay Kay Klein.

In describing the achievements of the great science fiction minds, it is important to fully examine the thought process as well as the summation of ideas given to society.

In my novel *Voyage of the Space Beagle*, I created a character whom I described as a Nexialist. *Nexialism* is my own term for "applied whole-ism," or a mental and scientific discipline with the culmination of a definite solution achieved through the bringing together and integration of many sciences.

Pioneering science fiction authors of the early to middle 20th century were developing and excelling in their processes. John W. Campbell had his anthropological aspects of science fiction. Edmond Hamilton, Leigh Brackett, Edward Elmer Smith, and Ray Cummings were involved in developing the first of the space operas. Jack Williamson, Stanley G. Weinbaum, L. Sprague de Camp, and Harry Bates were all busy developing their own personalities within science fiction. I as well had started my exploration of non-Aristotelian philosophy and Sir Alfred Korzybski's General Semantics, which in turn helped me to develop *The World of Null-A* and other stories.

But while we were all examining the universe through our own perspectives and disciplines, there was Forrest J Ackerman who had been around since the very first days of the pulps. Forrest Ackerman is a 20th-century Nexialist of science fiction, hyperactive as author, editor, anthologist, agent, publisher, actor, lecturer, archivist, historian, and fan. But more than just delving deeply into each of these activities, Forrest J Ackerman has been able to successfully take the very essence of each of them and in his lifetime to present his world, *our* worlds in such a fashion as to allow the greatest number of people—already hungry for a feast that could satiate their imaginations—to immerse themselves into the very heart and soul of what science fiction is here for: to say to the world that there is not just one solution to future problems and opportunities, or two solutions, but unlimited possibilities in ideas and disciplines.

PREFACE

Forrest J Ackerman, Graduate with Honors, The Nexialist Foundation

BY A. E. VAN VOGT

Several years after Forrest J Ackerman was introduced to the first pulp magazine in 1926, he started the first correspondence club for kids. By the age of 15 he was actively corresponding with over 100 fans from every part of the globe.

In his colorful lifetime he has met and befriended the likes of H. G. Wells; Edgar Rice Burroughs of the *Tarzan* and *John Carter of Mars* adventures; Hugo Gernsback, the publisher/editor of *Amazing Stories* (the premier science fiction pulp magazine); Frank R. Paul, the fantastic artist of the pulps who first gave us highly imaginative, full-color renderings of life on other star systems; artist Virgil Finlay; authors Henry Kuttner and Catherine Moore; Frederik Pohl; and scores of other science fiction authors, artists, and editors.

Forrest J Ackerman has himself edited numerous science fiction anthologies and has had over four dozen stories published, while being the literary representative of authors such as Harry Bates, whose immortal story "Farewell to the Master" became the classic science fiction film *The Day the Earth Stood Still*; Ray Cummings; Raymond F. Jones, author of "This Island Earth" and so much more; Leslie F. Stone; and, amongst a couple of hundred others, myself over a period spanning more than 40 years.

Forrest J Ackerman has participated in 54 of the 55 World Science Fiction Conventions around the world, including the very first. He has been a guest of honor all around the United States and Canada, but more importantly, Forry has been a sort of diplomatic representative of science fiction to other countries and cultures, including Australia, Brazil, the Czech Republic, England, France, Germany, Hungary, Italy, Japan, Portugal, Russia, Scandinavia, and Spain. In the late

In the '40s and '50s, every space in a movie theater was used to advertise—something. As one left, the transom above the door to the street was plastered with what were called "banners" advertising upcoming shows. It was a great period for sci-fi films, and I was able to collect some unique mementos from these films.

1990s, he was a guest of honor at the International Conference on Science Fiction in Beijing, China.

Even at home, Forrest J Ackerman is adding members to the legion of science fiction. For the past 45 years, he has guided 25,000 fans through a tour of his 18-room Ackermansion, which sits up near the Griffith Park Observatory. And he continues to make his home the home of many fans on an almost weekly basis at no cost to the public, in order to spread the good will of science fiction and the imagination.

(Standing, left to right) Ultima, Robby, and Gort. (Kneeling) Forry.

The late editor Anthony Boucher said of him, "If Forrest J Ackerman had not lived, it would have been necessary to invent him." George Pal, producer and special-effects man of films such as *Destination Moon* and *War of the Worlds*, is credited with having called Ackerman's collection "the Fort Knox of science fiction." No human being (if indeed Mr. Ackerman is human and not simply an alien in disguise) has ever been so intimately involved in all aspects of science fiction. How fortunate that this octogenarian's almost eidetic memory is amazingly intact.

So enjoy this phenomenal volume in which Forrest J Ackerman, Nexialist of the science fiction realm, allows us to examine through his eyes the highlights of a century of imagination and wonder, so that we may all be inspired to continue.

My first visit to Forrest J Ackerman's house was with Rick Baker in 1972.

Rick and I had made a silly monster movie called *Schlock*, through which we had met FJA in his role as editor of the magazine *Famous Monsters of Filmland*.

The house, off Olympic Boulevard near La Cienega, was stuffed with science fiction and fantasy memorabilia. The amazing collection of books, posters, stills, toys, and props spilled onto and into everything—even the refrigerator.

Later, when FJA moved into the "Ackermansion" (the former Jon Hall estate) in "Horrorwood, Karloffornia," I found myself helping them schlep countless boxes of treasures into the Hollywood Hills.

The extraordinary Ackerman collection benefited from his countless friendships, not only with the leading lights of fantasy literature, but with movie folk, going back to Carl Laemmle himself.

His boyhood chums include Ray Harryhausen and Ray Bradbury. Friends and acquaintances like George Pal, Fritz Lang, Robert Bloch, Bela Lugosi, Vincent Price, Joe Dante, Dick Smith, Ib Melchior, Mrs. Willis O'Brien, and Curt Siodmak contributed the books and props that make up his remarkable collection.

Forrest J Ackerman published the first known list of fantastic films (all 34 that he was aware of) in 1932. Sixty-five years later, he is still keeping track.

Forrest J Ackerman is many things. He is a literary agent. An actor. A fan. An author. A punster. An editor. An anthologist. A publisher. A collector. An eminently qualified person to write about *The World of Science Fiction*. And a dear, dear friend.

In 1972, a 22-year-old former 20th Century Fox mailroom guy named John Landis made his first $60,000 feature film, *Schlock*. I loved it. Originally filmed under the title *The Banana Monster*, it was given a limited release but was so popular, it made $6 million. This 40" x 60" poster is one of the few that exist today.

John Landis
Los Angeles, 1997

THIS VOLUME IS DEDICATED
TO THE MEMORY OF

Alden and Wendayne Ackerman
Isaac Asimov & Harry Bates
Edgar Rice Burroughs
John W. Campbell
Mark Carducci
Stanton A. Coblentz & Ray Cummings
Gerry de la Ree & E. Everett Evans
Georges Gallet & Hugo Gernsback
Brigitte Helm & Linus Hogenmiller
David H. Keller & Henry Kuttner
Fritz Lang
Catherine L. Moore & Morojo
Sam Moskowitz & George Pal
Frank R. Paul
Claude Rains & Gene Roddenberry
Conrad H. Ruppert
Carl Sagan & Edward E. Smith
John Taine & William F. Temple
A. Hyatt Verrill
Stanley G. Weinbaum &
Herbert George Wells
Belle & George Herbert Wyman
Ludwig "Esperanto" Zamenhof

AND AMONG THE LIVING TO

Jacqueline Connors Appelbaum
Dennis Billows & Ray Bradbury
Anthony Brzezinski & Arthur C. Clarke
John L. Coker III
Walt & Mary Ellen Daugherty
Mr & Mrs L. Sprague de Camp
Walter Ernsting
Brian Forbes
Stuart Gardner
Kristina Hallind
Ion Hobana
Charles D. Hornig
Alex Kill Family & David Kyle Family
Robert Madle
Tom & Terri Pinckard
Mr & Mrs Frederik Pohl
Julius Schwartz & Curt Siodmak
Jack Speer & Olaf Stapledon
Takumi & Tetsu
Bjo Trimble
A.E. van Vogt & Peter Vollmann
Harry Warner Jr. & Jack Williamson

AND MY PUBLISHER,
W. Quay Hays

Forry's introduction to "scientifiction."

INTRODUCTION

In the Beginning

T he wizard of words, Ray Bradbury, has called October "the wild, the eerie month." It was in October—of 1926 to be precise— that I, little 9-year-old Forry Ackerman, with wide, wondering eyes, received the Halloween gift that would influence, orient, and govern my entire life. Standing in front of a newsstand at the northeast corner of Santa Monica and Western Boulevards in Los Angeles, the October issue of *Amazing Stories* jumped off the magazine rack, grabbed hold of me, and spoke to me. It said, "Take me home, little boy. You will *love* me!"

And thus began a lifelong love affair with science fiction, although at the time it was known by the portmanteau coinage of "scientifiction." It would not popularly become "science fiction" until 1929.

That October, I had just seen my first circus and had been amazed by the variety of animal life-forms: those trunk-curling jungle pachyderms, the elephants; the ferocious felines of the cat family—lions, tigers, leopards; the great lumbering rhinos and hippos; the long-necked giraffes; and the humanoid anthropoids—apes.

And now, on the cover of this *Amazing Stories,* what did my popping orbs behold? It was some kind of upright crustacean creature about three times the size of a human being, greeting a man in what seemed to be a friendly gesture. The human in ragged torn clothes had apparently just emerged from a futuristic submarine. Austrian artist Frank Rudolph Paul had captured my soul.

Inside, I learned that the cover illustrated a scene from "Beyond the Pole" by A. Hyatt Verrill, one of the

Little Forry Ackerman in his pre–sci-fi days.

(Above) My first of many sci-fi–obsessed correspondents was Linus Hogenmiller (above), shown here in 1930. (Opposite) Robert A. W. Lowndes and "4sJ" in "futuristicostume," New York City, July 4, 1939.

pioneering authors of magazine science fiction. Upon reading "A Columbus of Space" by astronomer/writer Garrett P. Serviss, I learned of the planet Venus and realized for the first time that Earth was not the only world circling our sun. The third story, "The Purchase of the North Pole," was my introduction to the fabulous Frenchman Jules Verne; that story was followed by H. G. Wells's mutated creatures on "The Island of Dr. Moreau," which in 1932 would become the silver screen "manimals" of *Island of Lost Souls* (featuring Charles Laughton). Editor Hugo Gernsback's "sugar-coated science" had opened my eyes to all sorts of wonders I had never imagined.

As I reflect upon that first issue, I wonder how much of it I could have understood, as I had never before heard of atoms or comets or zodiacal light, or epiphytes or vivisection or colored undulations, or a multitude of other words to be found in "scientifiction" stories. But I was not afraid to consult the dictionary or to ask my elders. And I couldn't get enough.

One page had a fascinating ad for a novel of "700 years hence," *Ralph 124C 41+*, "a Romance of the year 2660," by Hugo Gernsback with a jacket by the afore-mentioned Frank R. Paul (see page 79). It showed the high-domed Ralph, the greatest living scientist of that distant future, what today we would call "faxing" a message to his sweetheart, visible live and life-size before his eyes on an oval "visiscope" screen. The $2.15 purchase price (postpaid) might as well have been $215 for a book today, so although I "faunched" for it (a fan's word for craving something passionately), it would be some years before I could afford a copy.

Gernsback's editorial shaped my personal aesthetic to such a degree that it is only fitting that I reprint it here, word for word, in its entirety. Just flip the page. Welcome, then, old fans and novices, to *Forrest J Ackerman's World of Science Fiction*.

April, 1926   25 Cents

AMAZING STORIES

HUGO GERNSBACK
EDITOR

Stories By

H. G. WELLS

JULES VERNE

EDGAR ALLEN POE

EXPERIMENTER PUBLISHING COMPANY, NEW YORK, PUBLISHERS OF
RADIO NEWS - SCIENCE & INVENTION - RADIO REVIEW - AMAZING STORIES - RADIO INTERNACIONAL

Volume
1

THE
MAGAZINE
OF
SCIENTIFICTION

April, 1926
No. 1.

HUGO GERNSBACK, F.R.S., *Editor*
DR. T. O'CONOR SLOANE, M.A., Ph.D.; *Managing Editor*
Editorial and General Offices - - - 53 Park Place, New York, N. Y.

Extravagant Fiction Today - - - - - - *Cold Fact Tomorrow*

A NEW SORT OF MAGAZINE

By HUGO GERNSBACK, F.R.S.

NOTHER fiction magazine!
At first thought it does seem impossible that there could be room for another fiction magazine in this country. The reader may well wonder, "Aren't there enough already, with the several hundreds now being published?" True. But this is not "another fiction magazine," AMAZING STORIES is a *new* kind of fiction magazine! It is entirely new—entirely different—something that has never been done before in this country. Therefore, AMAZING STORIES deserves your attention and interest.

There is the usual fiction magazine, the love story and the sex-appeal type of magazine, the adventure type, and so on, but a magazine of "Scientifiction" is a pioneer in its field in America.

By "scientifiction" I mean the Jules Verne, H. G. Wells, and Edgar Allan Poe type of story—a charming romance intermingled with scientific fact and prophetic vision. For many years stories of this nature were published in the sister magazines of AMAZING STORIES—"SCIENCE & INVENTION" and "RADIO NEWS."

But with the ever increasing demands on us for this sort of story, and more of it, there was only one thing to do—publish a magazine in which the scientific fiction type of story will hold forth exclusively. Toward that end we have laid elaborate plans, sparing neither time nor money.

Edgar Allan Poe may well be called the father of "scientifiction." It was he who really originated the romance, cleverly weaving into and around the story, a scientific thread. Jules Verne, with his amazing romances, also cleverly interwoven with a scientific thread, came next. A little later came H. G. Wells, whose scientifiction stories, like those of his forerunners, have become famous and immortal.

It must be remembered that we live in an entirely new world. Two hundred years ago, stories of this kind were not possible. Science, through its various branches of mechanics, electricity, astronomy, etc., enters so intimately into all our lives today, and we are so much immersed in this science, that we have become rather prone to take new inventions and discoveries for granted. Our entire mode of living has changed with the present progress, and it is little wonder, therefore, that many fantastic situations—impossible 100 years ago—are brought about today.

It is in these situations that the new romancers find their great inspiration.

Not only do these amazing tales make tremendously interesting reading—they are also always instructive. They supply knowledge that we might not otherwise obtain—and they supply it in a very palatable form. For the best of these modern writers of scientifiction have the knack of imparting knowledge, and even inspiration, without once making us aware that we are being taught.

And not only that! Poe, Verne, Wells, Bellamy, and many others have proved themselves real prophets. Prophesies made in many of their most amazing stories are being realized—and have been realized. Take the fantastic submarine of Jules Verne's most famous story, "Twenty Thousand Leagues Under the Sea" for instance. He predicted the present day submarine almost down to the last bolt! New inventions pictured for us in the scientifiction of today are not at all impossible of realization tomorrow. Many great science stories destined to be of an historical interest are still to be written, and AMAZING STORIES magazine will be the medium through which such stories will come to you. Posterity will point to them as having blazed a new trail, not only in literature and fiction, but in progress as well.

We who are publishing AMAZING STORIES realize the great responsibility of this undertaking, and will spare no energy in presenting to you, each month, the very best of this sort of literature there is to offer.

Exclusive arrangements have already been made with the copyright holders of the entire voluminous works of ALL of Jules Verne's immortal stories. Many of these stories are not known to the general American public yet. For the first time they will be within easy reach of every reader through AMAZING STORIES. A number of German, French and English stories of this kind by the best writers in their respective countries, have already been contracted for and we hope very shortly to be able to enlarge the magazine and in that way present always more material to our readers.

How good this magazine will be in the future is up to you. Read AMAZING STORIES—get your friends to read it and then write us what you think of it. We will welcome constructive criticism—for only in this way will we know how to satisfy you.

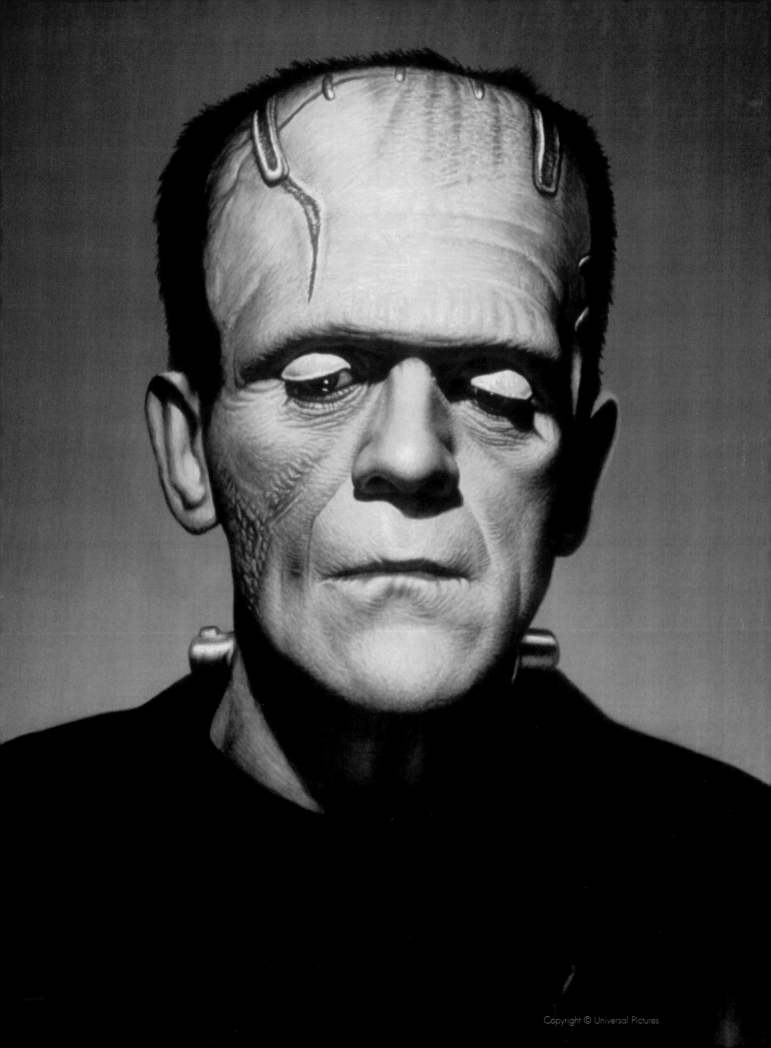

CHAPTER ONE
The Maid Who Made a Monster
Mary Shelley's *Frankenstein*

Brian W. Aldiss, second only to Arthur C. Clarke as the best-known British author of modern science fiction, has characterized Mary Wollstonecraft Shelley as "the Mother of Science Fiction." And in the science fiction community, the appellation has pretty much stuck.

Her claim to fame is the novel *Frankenstein*, written in 1818 when she was in her late teens. Inspired by German ghost stories that she and her friends had been reading during the unusually wet summer of 1816, Mary had a nightmare one stormy night in Switzerland, which galvanized her imagination. She developed the world-famous novel titled *Frankenstein; or, The Modern Prometheus*. One wonders why she didn't at least call it *Dr. Frankenstein*. Today, the name usually conjures up not the anatomist but the creature played by Boris Karloff in the classic 1931 film, and this is largely due to the brilliant work of makeup master Jack Pierce, who created that pasty face, scarred forehead, and bolted neck. However, there were a number of Frankenstein films, starting in 1957 with *The Curse of Frankenstein*, that were directed by Terence Fisher and that starred Peter Cushing as the infamous doctor; these films are noteworthy because they focus on Frankenstein the man, not his monster.

There are more than 250 editions of the book: illustrated editions; foreign editions (German, French, Dutch, Spanish, Italian, Portuguese, Japanese, Greek); sequels (*The Bride of*

The most familiar visage in all of literature (not just sci-fi) undoubtedly belongs to the Frankenstein monster, introduced in 1931 by Boris Karloff, with makeup designed by Jack Pierce.

Mary Wollstonecraft Shelley (1797–1851) was in her late teens when she wrote her novel *Frankenstein; or, the Modern Prometheus*. Despite the fact that her name does not appear prominently on the three-volume first edition of 1818 (far right), her creation ensured her a place in history (the portrait above was painted in 1841 by Rothwell and is in the National Portrait Gallery in London, England). So many editions of the book have appeared over the years that I have an entire cabinet full of them (right). On the following pages are some editions from around the world.

Frankenstein); spin-offs; and dozens of spoofs (including *Slave of Frankenstein, Pet of Frankenstein, Rivals of Frankenstein, The Frankenstein Diaries, Burlesque of Frankenstein, Frankenstein's Aunt,* and *Frankenstein Is Alive and Well and Living with Mrs. Frankenstein*).

THE STORY

The jacket blurb on the Wordsworth Classics of England edition sums up the story succinctly. "The monster is created by galvanism from human remains by a young student of Natural Philosophy called Frankenstein. The monstrous creation inspires revulsion in all he encounters despite a desperate and pathetic desire for affection, sympathy, understanding and a mate. This rejection leads to the unfolding of a classic Gothic tale of terror with death, insanity bred of grief, destruction and a chilling pursuit which culminates in a terrible nemesis in the frozen Arctic wastes." Sounds pretty exciting, doesn't it?

Here's where I'll commit heresy, at the risk of being banished to Blasphemer's Plateau by the scholars, the cognoscenti. I must confess that I've never found the story to live up to its promise. Perhaps in 1818 it was more shocking, but today it's intolerably dull.

First of all, the description of the monster is way too brief. He has watery yellow eyes that match his yellow skin. His complexion is shriveled, his lips straight and black. "No mortal could support the horror of that countenance. A mummy again endued with animation could not be so hideous as that wretch. His skin scarcely covered the work of muscles and arteries beneath; his hair was of a lustrous black, and flowing; his teeth of a pearly whiteness. A thing such as even Dante could not

have conceived." And that's about it. One wonders how Edgar Allan Poe might have described him. Or H. P. Lovecraft? Robert Bloch? Stephen King? Shelley may be the Mother of Science Fiction, but is she a master?

Second, the monster does not dominate the book; he makes an occasional appearance.

Finally, the denouement never seems to have bothered anyone else but leaves me incredulous. If I were to set out today for the Frozen Ocean of the north, a relatively normal-looking human being with plenty of cash in my pocket and the ability to ask questions and purchase tickets and meals, I wouldn't be able to get there without a lot of civilized assistance. So how did this penniless monstrosity, from whom everyone cringes in

MEXICAN

JAPANESE

SPANISH

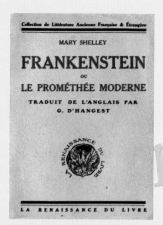

FRENCH

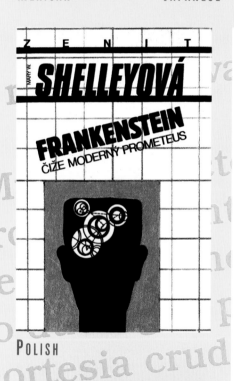

POLISH

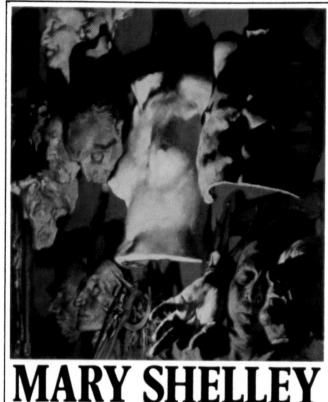

MARY SHELLEY FRANKENSTEIN

oder Der moderne Prometheus
Mit einem Essay von Norbert Kohl
insel taschenbuch

NEW ZEALAND

GERMAN

MARY SHELLEY
FRANKENSTEIN

introduzione di Laura Caretti

OSCAR
MONDADORI

A Marvel Illustrated Novel

$8.95
CAN. $9.95

MARY WOLLSTONECRAFT SHELLEY'S
FRANKENSTEIN

illustrated by BERNI WRIGHTSON

introduction by
STEPHEN KING

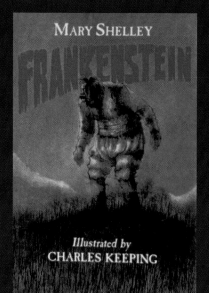

MARY SHELLEY

FRANKENSTEIN

Illustrated by
CHARLES KEEPING

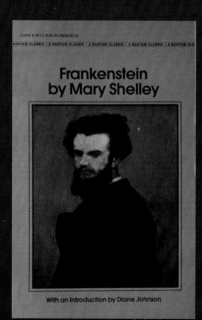

Frankenstein
by Mary Shelley

With an Introduction by Diane Johnson

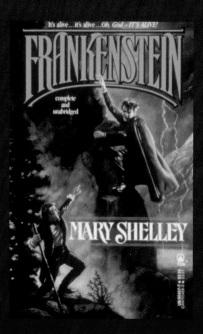

It's alive…it's alive…*Oh, God—IT'S ALIVE!*

FRANKENSTEIN

complete
and
unabridged

MARY SHELLEY

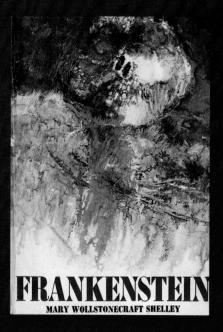

FRANKENSTEIN
MARY WOLLSTONECRAFT SHELLEY

Shelley's story has spawned countless spin-offs,
including The Adult Version of Frankenstein (1970), a sexploitation
adaptation by Hal Kantor (below).

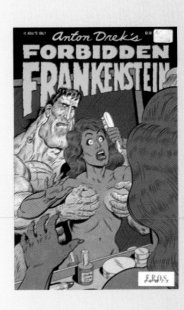

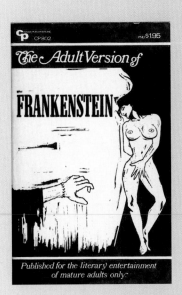

terror at his sight, manage three meals a day and passage on coaches, trains, a ship, whatever it took to traverse so great a distance?

Nevertheless, I expect it will go on being published and republished and I'll have collected over 300 volumes before my life is through. And if there is an afterlife (which, as a card-carrying secular humanist in the distinguished company of Isaac Asimov and Gene Roddenberry, I have long doubted) and I meet up with Mary Shelley at such time, I will certainly ask her forgiveness for being so critical of her classic. *I* should write something that gets read for 200 years. Hopefully she'll explain to me how the monster made it to the frozen Arctic wastes.

These two frame enlargements from the 16-minute 1910 *Frankenstein* film by the Edison Company give you some idea of the static nature of the adaptation. In both scenes, the monster (Charles Ogle) grapples with the doctor (played by Augustus Fuller). On the right, they are fighting in Dr. Frankenstein's honeymoon suite (that's the bride lying on the floor).

FRANKENSTEIN ON FILM

When a film called *Frankenstein's Trestle* was discovered to have been made around the turn of the century, it was believed for years to have been the first known filmic depiction of Mary Shelley's novel. However, it was eventually learned that it had nothing to do with the man-made monster; Frankenstein was simply the name of a town with a trestle.

But in 1910, the Edison Company (as in Thomas Alva) did make a film called *Frankenstein* and, fortunately, that version still exists. Many years ago, in my home in the company of Don ("*Frankenstein* expert") Glut and Bill ("Keep Watching the Skies!") Warren, a collector with a print of the film projected it for me. At 975 feet, it's only 16 minutes long, and the monster, played by Charles Ogle, is ludicrous in appearance. Nevertheless it was a thrill to see this *Frankenstein* film from nearly 90 years ago. When its owner left with the reel of film, one of my friends drove him to the hotel where he was staying and reported to me afterward that the collector had put a pistol on top of the can containing the film! Through the years, he has tried to get the Academy of Motion Pictures to incorporate it in one of its Award performances, so far without success. I believe he wants five figures for its use.

A few years later, a version was made by director Joseph W. Smiley called *Life Without Soul* (1915). The monster was played by Percy Darrell Standing, a brother of the better-known actor Sir Guy Standing.

But it was the 1931 James Whale–directed version with Karloff that left a long-lasting impression on movie audiences. Made for a mere $250,000, the film grossed over $25 million—nothing to sneeze at for a film of the '30s. Pierce's makeup for the monster is copyrighted by Universal Studios, which is why Frankenstein movies from other studios have a monster that looks quite different, and why almost all the Universal monsters look alike.

The tale has been filmed repeatedly, and not just in the early days of

Above, a trade ad announcing Universal's intention of making a film of *Frankenstein* in 1930 (note that the film was to star Bela Lugosi as the monster). Below, a rare photograph of director James Whale dusting off Boris Karloff on the set of *Frankenstein* (1931).

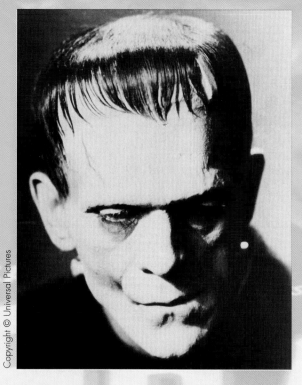

Copyright © Universal Pictures

Responsibility for the enormous worldwide success of *Frankenstein* has, from the beginning, been placed upon the performance of Boris Karloff as the monster. A 43-year-old at the time the film was shot, the former farmhand and truck driver's performance was so nuanced and touching, and the film so well constructed, the monster's actions so unpredictable, that he couldn't fail to make a huge impression with the public. Notice the change in billing he got from the original one-sheet (right) to that on a rerelease lobby card from the late '40s (below).

I think that the 1931 version of *Frankenstein* is still one of my favorite films, not only because it embraces three genres that often go hand-in-hand—science fiction, horror, and fantasy—but also because it does so in such an open, honest way. This sequence, where the monster first learns a human characteristic from a little girl, is where it all coalesces—intriguing, touching, and frightening all at once.

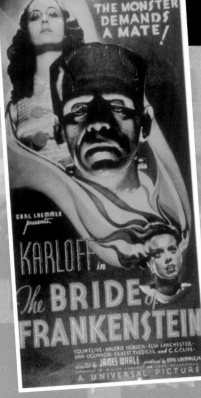

WARNING! THE MONSTER DEMANDS A MATE!

CARL LAEMMLE presents

KARLOFF in

The BRIDE of FRANKENSTEIN

COLIN CLIVE · VALERIE HOBSON · ELSA LANCHESTER · UNA O'CONNOR · ERNEST THESIGER · and O.P. HEGGIE

Directed by JAMES WHALE · produced by CARL LAEMMLE, Jr.

A UNIVERSAL PICTURE

Regia: ROWLAND V. LEE

JOSEPHINE HUTCHINSON

Boris Karloff and James Whale were persuaded by Universal to concoct a sequel to their *Frankenstein* smash hit, so they decided to continue the story of the novel by having Dr. Frankenstein create a *Bride of Frankenstein* (1935). The entire film leads us along to the moment where the bride (played by Elsa Lanchester) meets her intended—only to shriek in revulsion (top left)! It was around this time (1968) that I was able to meet Karloff (opposite page, bottom), who was being besieged by projects that could spin off the *Frankenstein* characters. In 1939, he starred in *Son of Frankenstein*, in which the character was so incidental to the story that many were disappointed, and he never played the monster again. This sense that the Frankenstein legend was being misused grew until well into the '50s. A 1957 painting/letter done by Los Angeles artist Burt Shonberg rhetorically asks the studios why they don't tell the story of the monster "the way it really happened."

The Maid Who Made a Monster: Mary Shelley's Frankenstein **49**

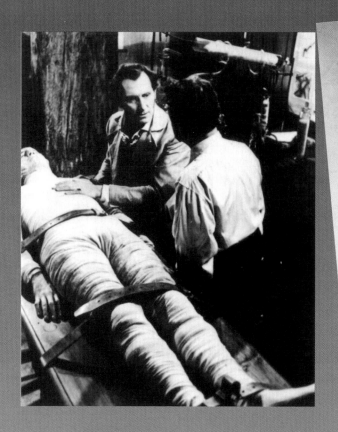

NEW AND GREATEST FRANKENSTEIN MONSTERPIECE!!

"THE REVENGE OF FRANKENSTEIN"

WE DARE YOU TO SEE IT!
WE DOUBLE-DARE YOU
TO FORGET IT!

If you go alone ...you'll find yourself running all the way home!

SUPER-NATURAL TECHNICOLOR

starring PETER CUSHING · EUNICE GAYSON · FRANCIS MATTHEWS · MICHAEL GWYNN

Written by JIMMY SANGSTER · Produced by ANTHONY HINDS · Directed by TERENCE FISHER · A HAMMER FILM PRODUCTION · A COLUMBIA PICTURE

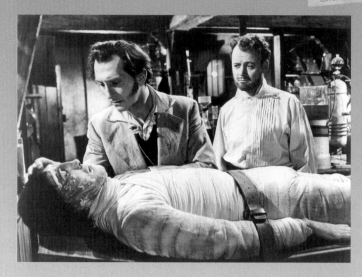

BORIS KARLOFF

FRANKENSTEIN 1970

TOM DUGGAN - IANA LUND

Regia di HOWARD W. KOCH distribuzione GOLD FILM

WIDESCREEN

WE DARE YOU TO SEE...

ANDY WARHOL'S FLESH FOR FRANKENSTEIN

ANDY WARHOL'S
FLESH FOR FRANKENSTEIN
starring JOE DALLESANDRO · UDO KIER · MONIQUE VAN VOOREN
introducing ARNO JUERGING · DALILA DI LAZZAR · SRDJAN ZELENOVIC

Music by CLAUDIO GIZZI · A Compagnia Cinematografica CHAMPION S.p.A. Rome production
Written and Directed by PAUL MORRISSEY · Produced by ANDREW BRAUNSBERG
EASTMANCOLOR · Distributed by EMI Film Distributors Ltd.

Reissues of the 1931 *Frankenstein* convinced producers that there was still plenty of box office in the story. *The Curse of Frankenstein* from 1957 (far left, top, middle, and bottom) was the first time Peter Cushing played the doctor (he would in five more films). They gave him some romantic interest, but it wasn't until *Frankenstein Created Woman* (left) that the doctor created a world-class looker (played by *Playboy* Playmate Susan Denberg). Not to be outdone, Boris Karloff got back into the act playing the doctor in such films as *Frankenstein 1970* (an Italian poster, above). They took the whole thing to the limit in 1973 with *Andy Warhol's Frankenstein* (right), originally presented in 3-D.

FAMOUS MONSTERS

#56 JULY

OF FILMLAND

A WARREN MAGAZINE

2 IN 1 ISSUE!

ALL ABOUT
**BORIS
KARLOFF**
HIS LIFE IN
PICTURES

COMMENTS ON
HIS DEATH BY

**CHRIS
LEE**

**PETER
LORRE**

**ELSA
LANCHESTER
FORREST
ACKERMAN

VINCENT
PRICE
LON CHANEY**

PLUS

"FRANKENSTEIN" COMPLETE WITH RARE PICTURES!!

FAMOUS MONSTERS #180

THE HORROR OF HALLOWEEN II
ON PAGE 12

FAMOUS MONSTERS

WARREN MAGAZINE

JAN. 1982

$2.00

**AMERICAN
WEREWOLF
IN LONDON
INTERVIEWS!**

**LINDA BLAIR'S
HELL NIGHT!**

THE GRIM REAPER
YOU'RE ON HIS MENU!

**THE MAD
GHOUL!** SEE PAGE 44

FORREST J ACKERMAN,

FAMOUS

MONSTER

OF FILMLAND

$10.95

BEST
BOOK
EVER!

The Behind-the-Screams
Story of Horrorwood's
First Filmonster Magazine
Bloch...Chaneys...Elvira...
Karloff...King...Lorre...
Lugosi...Reed...Savini...
Tor...More!

SEE—
A SPECIAL ALUMNI
FEARBOOK SECTION

SEE—
INSIDE THE ACKERMANSION

GRAVEYARD EXAMINER II

YOU AXED FOR IT AGAIN!

**Introduction by
VINCENT PRICE**

COLLECTOR'S EDITION

FAMOUS
MONSTERS

AUGUST

A WARREN MAGAZINE   PDC $1.25

100th GREAT ISSUE

THE
WORLD'S FIRST
**MONSTER
FAN**
MAGAZINE

Famous Monsters of Filmland — NEW! SPECIAL ISSUE — THE WORLD'S FIRST MONSTER FAN MAGAZINE — 1965 YEARBOOK

MONSTER WORLD — JAN. NO. 6 — 35¢ — HAVE A COOL YULE WITH A GHOUL IN THIS HORRIFIC HOLIDAY ISSUE! PLUS REVENGE of the ZOMBIES and RETURN of the VAMPIRE

STAR WARS RARE PIX! page 16 — WARREN MAGAZINE — FAMOUS MONSTERS #140 — WAR OF THE WORLDS—REFOUGHT! WHEN WORLDS COLLIDE—AGAIN! THE INCREDIBLE FILMS TO COME — THE MOST HELLISH FRANKENSTEIN

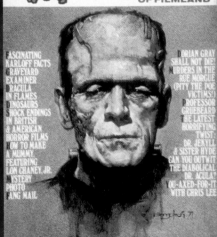

FAMOUS MONSTERS OF FILMLAND #94 — FASCINATING KARLOFF FACTS, GRAVEYARD EXAMINER, DRACULA IN FLAMES, DINOSAURS, SHOCK ENDINGS IN BRITISH & AMERICAN HORROR FILMS, HOW TO MAKE A MUMMY, FEATURING LON CHANEY, JR. MYSTERY PHOTO, FANG MAIL — DORIAN GRAY SHALL NOT DIE! MURDERS IN THE RUE MORGUE (PITY THE POE VICTIMS!) PROFESSOR GRUEBEARD, THE LATEST HORRIFYING TWIST! DR. JEKYLL & SISTER HYDE, CAN YOU OUTWIT THE DIABOLICAL DR. ACULA? YOU-AXED-FOR-IT WITH CHRIS LEE

FAMOUS MONSTERS OF FILMLAND AUGUST 196_ No.13 — 50¢ — BEST ISSUE EVER! 100 PAGES! COLLECTOR'S 13th ANNIVERSARY EDITION

FAMOUS MONSTERS OF FILMLAND — SURPRISE ISSUE! 32 EXTRA PAGES. BETTER THAN EVER — FEBRUARY 1963 — 50¢ — NEW-PHOTO FILMBOOK BRIDE OF FRANKENSTEIN — ROUTE 6_ HORROR SHO_

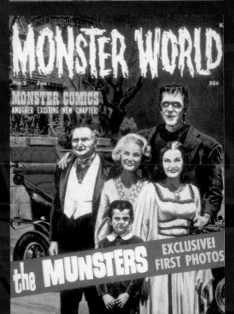

MONSTER WORLD — 35¢ — MONSTER COMICS ANOTHER EXCITING NEW CHAPTER — the MUNSTERS EXCLUSIVE! FIRST PHOTOS

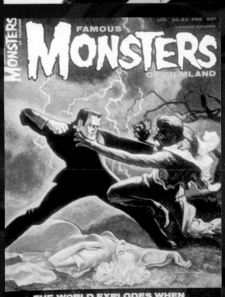

FAMOUS MONSTERS OF FILMLAND — JAN. NO. 42 — THE WORLD EXPLODES WHEN FRANKENSTEIN MEETS THE WOLFMAN ...SPECIAL IN THIS ISSUE

The 1960s were the heyday for my magazine *Famous Monsters of Filmland*. It seemed like "the kids" just couldn't get enough of monsters and ghouls, so it shouldn't be surprising that the most famous monster would grace our cover so many times. And when he did, that issue would outsell all the others for that year by a long shot. The longevity of *Famous Monsters* is one thing, but the longevity of the Frankenstein monster is something else again! James Warren was the Forry-sighted publisher.

Universal Studios

Universal City, California

Frankenstein mania really got a big boost in the early '60s when Universal decided to make him the unofficial mascot of their tour operations (providing employment to every tall actor in Hollywood, including Richard Keil in a photo taken during a live show on the tour, above right). Universal used Frankie as the centerpiece of a makeup show (opposite page, center), and marketed "Monster" trading cards. It wasn't the first Frankenstein-related product, and it won't be the last!

12 FRANKENSTEIN

MONSTER

© 1964 by Universal Picture Co., Inc.

ACULA

MONSTER BALLS
FAMOUS MONSTERS FROM
FAVORITE HORROR MOV
FRANKENSTEIN

FRANKENFORRY

INNOC
BLO

shelley

VIEW-M
FRANKENSTEIN

IN IS A MAN OF PARTS!

Hollywood: In the 1970s alone, more than 40 years after Karloff, audiences tuned in to the hugely successful NBC miniseries starring Michael Sarrazin (1973), delighted to Mel Brooks's classic spoof *Young Frankenstein* (1974), and were jolted by *Andy Warhol's Frankenstein* (in 3-D, also in 1974).

Upon its release, *Warhol's* was rated X for its sexually explicit content and medical gore. By today's standards, it could still offend but hardly shock. In an interesting, post–World War II twist, the obsessed scientist is trying to find a head and brain for his perfect male zombie to complement his already created female zombie. Together, the mad doctor insists, they will procreate and begin the perfect Serbian (read Aryan) race. He wants to find a male who epitomizes virility, so he waits outside a local bordello to stalk his victim. Two men leave together—one, an oversexed frequent patron who is precisely the type the doctor desires; the other, his buddy who has little interest in sex, is about to become a monk, and is there solely because of peer pressure. In short, the doctor beheads the wrong chap, his experiment fails, and everything that could go wrong *does*. Not for all tastes, by any means, but not worth completely dismissing either. And no Arctic journeys.

Mel Brooks—hot on the heels of his wildly successful parody of westerns, *Blazing Saddles*—opted next to satirize the conventions of the Frankenstein movies with his *Young Frankenstein*. Released during the 1974 Christmas season, the film was an enormous hit with hilarious performances by Gene Wilder (far left) as Dr. Frankenstein ("that's Franken*schteen*"); Peter Boyle as the monster; and Madeline Kahn (above left with Wilder), as well as Marty Feldman, Cloris Leachman, Teri Garr, and Kenneth Mars.

Young Frankenstein actors (left to right) Marty Feldman, Cloris Leachman, Gene Wilder, and Teri Garr.

Most recently, the box office flop *Mary Shelley's Frankenstein* (1995) was directed and produced by its star, Kenneth Branagh (he played the doctor; Robert De Niro played the monster).

Shelley's story has gone a long way, quite further than she ever could have imagined. Who can doubt that new scientific advances and political trends will yield further reinterpretations? I am sure that writers, directors, and audiences will continue to stay tuned in; I only hope that they go back to Karloff and recognize what an awesome film it was in its time.

England's top-ranking male stage performer, Kenneth Branagh (above and near right with Helena Bonham Carter), after making several successful films, was given $70 million to film his vision of *Mary Shelley's Frankenstein*. Despite (or perhaps because of) several truly shocking and horrifying moments (including a radical approach to the appearance of the monster, played by Robert De Niro, opposite page), the film failed with the public, and with me.

CHAPTER TWO
Prophets and Pioneers
Major Authors of Science Fiction

In 1902, French director Georges Méliès took us on *A Trip to the Moon (Le Voyage dans la Lune)*. In 1995, American director Ron Howard gave us *Apollo 13*. The former film was science fiction; the latter was history.

Therein lies the beauty of science fiction: It is about the "what if" notion that sparks the imagination of children and adults alike. It is about dreams and possibilities, and it is about nightmares and forewarnings.

In the words of John Clute, author of *Science Fiction: The Illustrated Encyclopedia*, "One of the most foolish accusations made about SF is that it fails to predict the future. This is not what SF sets out to do. What SF does is train its readers to look to the future." It would therefore be unfair to suggest that a given science fiction writer is not great if he or she does not predict, for the genre is filled with wondrous, amazing, imaginative stories about other planets, other times, variations on plants and insects and mammals. But prescience—the ability to foresee events—is a compelling thread in the world of science fiction (note that *prescience = pre + science*) and some of the greatest sci-fi writers could actually be seen as great inventors, even if only on paper. They include Jules Verne, H. G. Wells, Hugo Gernsback, Curt Siodmak, Robert A. Heinlein, Aldous Huxley, and George Orwell.

This is not to minimize the contributions of other sci-fi pioneers. For instance, Isaac Asimov's "Three Laws of Robotics" (see page 67) may not be prescient, but they influenced every significant story about, and all editors and readers with any interest in, robots. And Harlan Ellison's use of randy language certainly catered to a broader marketplace while maintaining award-worthy standards.

Some authors have been included in this chapter—for instance, Keller, Kuttner and Moore, and Septama—because they have been sorely neglected as the decades have passed. Their stories may not have been adapted into Hollywood blockbusters, but these writers had a great way with paper and pen and imagination, and had great supporters in their time.

A portrait of H. G. Wells done by Neil Austin for *Famous Fantastic Mysteries*.

BRIAN W. ALDISS

1925-

Since his debut novel *Non-Stop* in 1958, Aldiss has produced some 30 novels of such consistent high quality on a range of topics so vast that in some ways he's in a class of his own—even though his name might not have the same marquee value as, let's say, Ray Bradbury or Arthur C. Clarke.

Non-Stop tells of a starship colonized by fantastic mutants; *The Primal Urge* (1961) explores tinkering with basic human sexual attraction; *Hothouse* (1962) reveals a growing sun and an intolerant Earth; *An Age* (1967) is a philosophical time-travel tale; *Barefoot in the Head* (1969) is about an LSD-inundated culture in postwar Europe written in a style that has been likened to James Joyce; and the trilogy comprised of *Helliconia Spring* (1982), *Helliconia Summer* (1983), and *Helliconia Winter* (1985) is a future history of a planet with two competing intelligent races; their evolution is observed by Earthlings.

Aldiss has also written many short stories; all of his *Best of* collections are splendid.

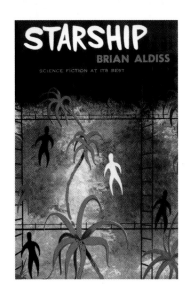

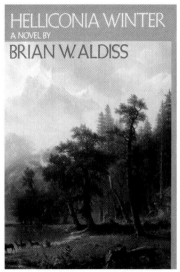

HELLICONIA
SUMMER

A NOVEL BY

BRIAN W. ALDISS

ISAAC ASIMOV

1920-1992

In 1939, *Amazing Stories* published Asimov's "Marooned Off Vesta," and the world would never be the same again. For more than five decades, Asimov proved to be the most relentless writer of the 20th century, publishing nearly 500 books—novels, short stories, children's books, essays,

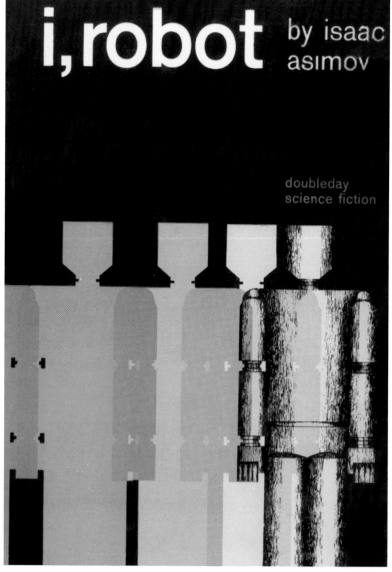

autobiographies. Science was his life, and science fiction was his passion. Like many other early pulp contributors, Asimov started out as a fan.

His story "Nightfall," published in 1941, is perhaps his most-read work. In it, the entire population of a perpetually sunlit planet goes mad when an eclipse brings on night for the first time in 2,000 years.

Asimov is the king of the robot writers: The novel *I, Robot* (1950) gave him a mainstream popularity that eluded many of his peers in the pulps. With the assistance of John W. Campbell Jr., who served as editor of *Astounding Stories* (later *Astounding Science Fiction* and *Analog Science Fiction–Science Fact*) from late 1937 to 1971, Asimov created the "Three Laws of Robotics":

1. A robot may not injure a human being, or through inaction, allow a human being to come to harm.
2. A robot must obey the orders given it by human beings except where such order would conflict with the First Law.
3. A robot must protect its own existence as long as such protection does not conflict with the First or Second Law.

These laws became a challenge to all other writers of robot stories. Perhaps no one could force a writer to adhere to them, but ultimately fans and editors would dismiss any writer who couldn't.

His *Foundation* trilogy—*Foundation* (1950), *Foundation and Empire* (1952), and *Second Foundation* (1953)—has maintained its popularity with sci-fi fans for almost 50 years, ensuring its status as the most popular written work ever produced in the genre. Whereas other futuristic stories written at the time tended to present human–alien interaction, Asimov focused on a solely human civilization. The tales are Asimov's allegorical take on the rise and fall of the Roman Empire, and it's safe to say that audiences love them because they are among the most thought-provoking fiction ever produced.

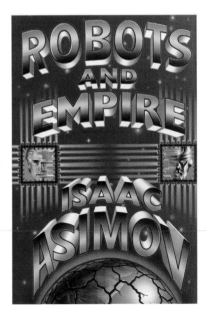

Asimov was a research chemist, a professor, an editor, and so much more. His nonfiction works dealt with genetics, biochemistry, technology, physics, astronomy, mythology—nothing was beyond his abilities. It was this informed nature that distinguished Asimov's science fiction from that of other pulp-fans-turned-author.

RAY BRADBURY

1920-

Bradbury is an astounding writer, although many of his works fall outside the realm of science fiction (some would argue that fantasy is his strong suit). But two of his most enduring works—*The Martian Chronicles* (1950) and *Fahrenheit 451* (1953)—are indisputable sci-fi landmarks.

The former is a collection of short stories written in the 1940s: Although there are definitely menacing Martians in the Bradbury canon, he is also credited with creating characters (whole families, in fact) whose Mars-based existence is not too dissimilar to ours on Earth. Some of the stories don't even focus on Martians, per se, but are about pioneer settlers on Mars.

The latter title is about a totalitarian U.S. government in which literary masterpieces must be burned, lest they threaten the political climate with their ideas and possibilities and solutions. The story's hero rebels and aspires to memorize all the great works for the sake of humanity.

His short story "The Fog Horn" became the film *The Beast from 20,000 Fathoms* (1953), which was the first project for special-effects genius Ray Harryhausen. "The Meteor" became *It Came from Outer Space* (also 1953), which he coscripted with David Schwartz. Perhaps his most significant Hollywood credit is as coscreenwriter (with John Huston) for the non–science fiction epic *Moby Dick* (1956), for which they won an Oscar.

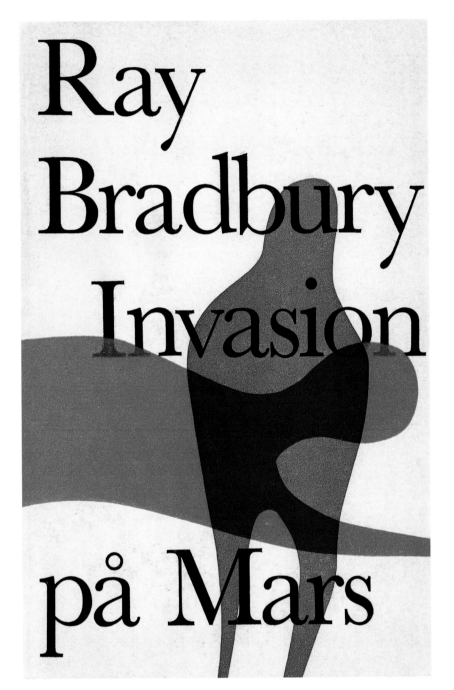

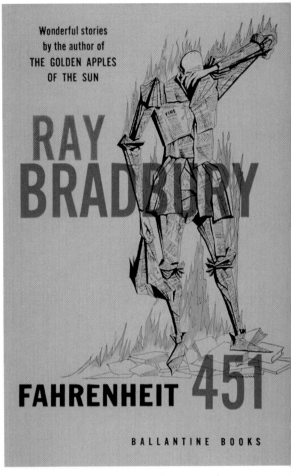

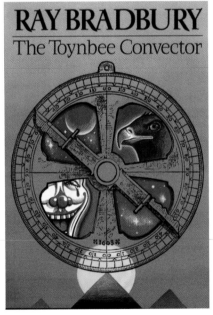

EDGAR RICE BURROUGHS

1875-1950

When his first novel was published in *All-Story* magazine in 1912, it was known as *Under the Moons of Mars*. Today it is known as *A Princess of Mars*. At the time of its initial publication, Burroughs felt that the story was so weird that his family might be embarrassed by having him identified as the author, so he created the double-entendre pseudonym Normal Bean (*bean* in 1912 referred to one's noggin; the pen name meant his head was on straight). Apparently, some editor didn't believe Normal was a normal name and changed it to Norman; thus the literary pun was lost.

In 1927, Hugo Gernsback tried an experiment. The editor issued *Amazing Stories Annual,* twice the size of the monthly and twice the price. He offered a scoop in the first publication of a brand-new "Barsoom" novel—complete—by Edgar Rice Burroughs: *The Master Mind of Mars.*

Burroughs is best known, of course, for the creation of Tarzan (White Skin, in the language of the jungle apes who raised him). Even the town of Tarzana, California, is named after his character. But before his epic writing career was through, he had transported millions of worldwide readers to

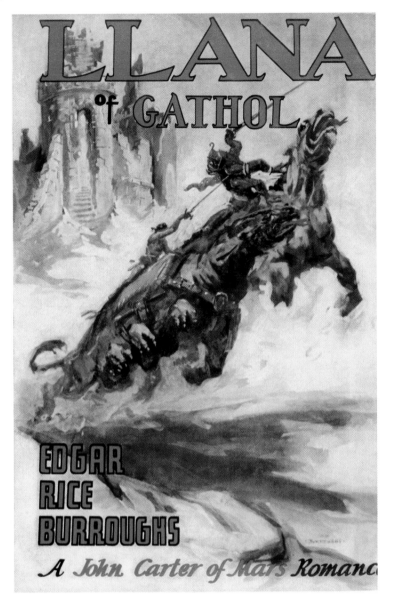

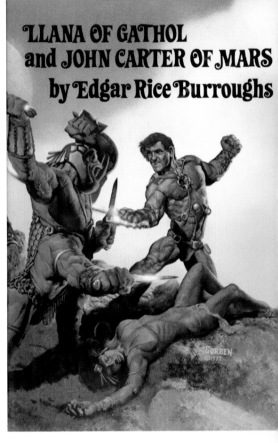

Mars (Barsoom), Venus (Amtor), the center of the Earth (Pellucidar), the moon, *The Land That Time Forgot* (1924), and even Atlantis. Burroughs is one of the few to have actually been translated into Esperanto (*La Princino de Marso* by Edgaro Rajs Buroz is better known as the aforementioned *A Princess of Mars*).

In 1975, a biography by Irwin Porges titled *Edgar Rice Burroughs, The Man Who Created Tarzan* was published; it was a monumental, fabulous, scholarly 819-page volume. According to Porges, Burroughs said not long before his death, "If there is a hereafter, I want to travel through space to visit the other planets."

During World War II, Cleve Cartmill wrote so realistically about the impending development of atomic power ("Deadline," *Astounding Science Fiction*, March 1944) that the publication's editor, John W. Campbell Jr., received a call from a military intelligence official. The government thought there had been a leak because the atomic details in Cartmill's fictional story were hitting too close to home. The author assured them it was simply educated extrapolation. The military wanted to forbid any additional stories with atomic speculation, fearing it would fortuitously offer information to the German enemy, but Campbell wisely convinced them that to suddenly cease publishing such stories would be a dead giveaway, since they had been a staple of the periodical for some years.

JOHN W. CAMPBELL JR.

1910-1971

During his 30-year-plus reign as editor of *Astounding Stories* (which he renamed *Astounding Science Fiction* in 1938 and *Analog Science Fiction–Science Fact* in 1960), the pulp won seven Hugo Awards for best sci-fi magazine. He is often credited with saving the genre as a whole by introducing excellent writers—including Isaac Asimov, Robert Heinlein, Clifford D. Simak, Theodore Sturgeon, and A. E. van Vogt—month after month to an enthusiastic, never-waning audience.

While still in his teens, Campbell sold his first story, "When the Atoms Failed," to *Amazing Stories* (published January 1930) during his sophomore year at the Massachusetts Institute of Technology. Under the pseudonym Don A. Stuart, he published a number of significant stories in the '30s, hitting one of many zeniths in 1938 with "Who Goes There?"—a story that is known to millions as Howard Hawks's classic sci-fi film, *The Thing* (1951). Director John Carpenter did an excellent remake in 1982, and an early episode of *The X-Files* ("Ice") was a remarkably close variation on the theme.

When he "graduated" from short stories and novelettes to novels, he soon became known as the rival of E. E. Smith in the genre of space operas, with works such as *The Mightiest Machine* (1947), *The Incredible Planet* (1949), and *Islands of Space* (1956). He also helped Asimov devise the "Three Laws of Robotics."

Campbell was guest of honor at the Fifth World Science Fiction Convention in 1947 in Philadelphia, at the 12th in 1954 in San Francisco, and at the 15th in London in 1957. His name may not be as familiar as Verne's or Bradbury's, but he's a seminal figure in the Golden Age of Science Fiction.

ARTHUR C. CLARKE

1917-

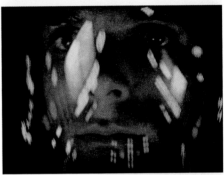

A SIGNET BOOK • Q3580 • 95c

2001 a space odyssey

A NOVEL BY **ARTHUR C. CLARKE**
BASED ON THE SCREENPLAY OF THE **MGM** FILM BY
STANLEY KUBRICK and ARTHUR C. CLARKE

2001 a space odyssey
is the history-making motion picture
produced and directed by Stanley Kubrick.
In Cinerama®

Clarke has built a career around speculations about technology. As early as 1945, he predicted the geosynchronous communication satellite in an article called "Extra-Terrestrial Relay" (*Wireless World* magazine). He is an accomplished physicist and mathematician with hundreds of nonfiction articles to his credit (in everything from the journal *Electronic Engineering* to *Playboy*), and he had his share of pulp fans in the '40s and '50s, but he undoubtedly made his biggest impression with *2001: A Space Odyssey* (1968). He wrote the screenplay with the film's director, Stanley Kubrick, and a novelization (same title) of the screenplay that same year. Both the book and film are classics.

One of the themes in *2001* is the questionable practice of creating artificial intelligence. HAL, the man-made computer that controls all functions of the spaceship, is arguably cinema's all-time most creepy character not played by a human. (An early episode of TV's *The X-Files* revisited the theme to chilling effect in the early '90s.) Another leitmotif—one found in much of Clarke's work—is the spiritual enlightenment of man in the face of adversity. What will be the fate of the lone surviving astronaut, and will his experience—unlike that of any other man, thereby putting him in an evolved class of his own—have been worth it? Clarke's favorite self-penned story ("Transit of Earth" from 1972) elaborates upon this same premise: A dying astronaut records man's first view from Mars of Earth crossing its sun; despite his failing life supports, the astronaut recognizes that it's a great moment for mankind.

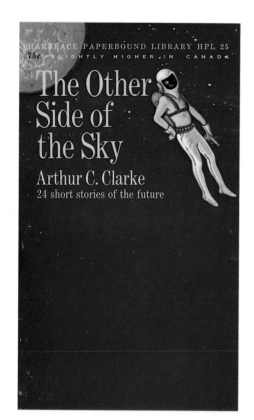

Clarke has produced around two dozen novels since the early '50s, not to mention many short-story collections, edited volumes, autobiographies, and lots of nonfiction. "The Star" won the 1956 Hugo Award for best short story. In 1962, the nonfiction *Interplanetary Flight: An Introduction to Astronautics* won a UNESCO award. *Rendezvous with Rama* (1973) won Campbell, Hugo, Jupiter, and Nebula Awards (an honor that had never, and has not since, been bestowed upon any one work). In the 1980s, Clarke wrote two *2001* sequels—*2010: Odyssey Two* (1982) and *2061: Odyssey Three* (1988).

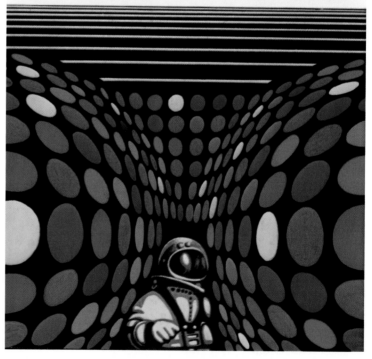

STANTON A. COBLENTZ

1896-1982

In addition to his accomplishments in poetry, Coblentz was an acclaimed sci-fi writer whose forte was social satire. He was a contributor to the pulps from the very beginning. One of his premier efforts was the classic *The Sunken World* (1928), in which modern submarines discover and ultimately disturb an Atlantean paradise; other important early works include "After 12,000 Years" (1929), "In Caverns Below" (1935), and "Into Plutonian Depths" (1931). *Moon People* (1964) addressed racial segregation. His last full-length novel was *The Island People* (1971).

Coblentz was a great humanitarian. When he died, he willed all additional royalties from his work to a children's institute for the blind in New York City.

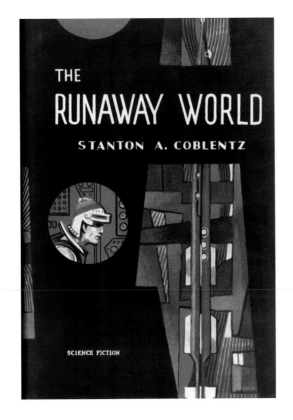

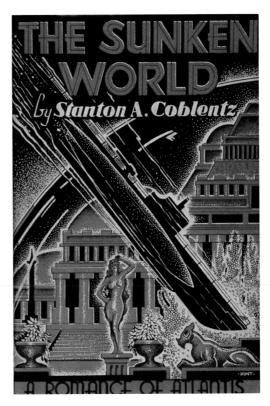

SIR ARTHUR CONAN DOYLE

1859-1930

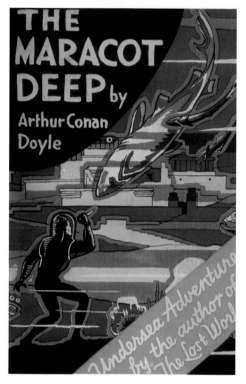

This Scottish doctor is best known for the Sherlock Holmes mysteries that he wrote between 1887 and 1927. But he also wrote *The Lost World* (1912), in which the prehistoric meets the modern world. This classic was filmed three times: with Wallace Beery as Professor Challenger in 1925, Claude Rains in 1960, and John Rhys-Davies in 1992. (Other than the dinosaurs, the story has nothing to do with Steven Spielberg's 1997 blockbuster, *The Lost World: Jurassic Park.*

In addition to the original *Lost World*, he gave the us some other Professor Challenger classics, notably the witty story "When the World Screamed" and the deadly serious novel *The Poison Belt.* His short story "The Great Keinplatz Experiment" has been heavily anthologized. His last story was the Atlantean tale "The Maracot Deep" (1929).

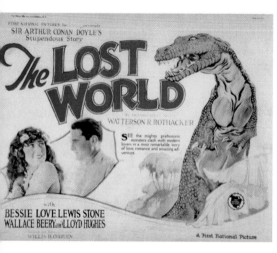

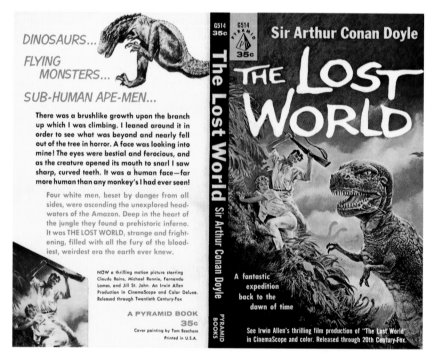

HARLAN ELLISON

1934-

Ellison insists he writes speculative fiction, which he refers to as "spec-fic." He curses the term "sci-fi," which I coined over four decades ago, with coruscating hate. He wishes me dead and the sooner the better; he has said so in a letter. Nonetheless, Ellison has been awarded more Hugos and Nebulas than any other author in the sci-fi/spec-fic field. His two best known works are "'Repent, Harlequin!' Said the Ticktockman," for which he won a 1966 Hugo Award, and "I Have No Mouth, and I Must Scream"—I consider these two of the most original titles in the history of the genre. "The Demon with the Glass Hand" (an *Outer Limits* segment) is his television classic.

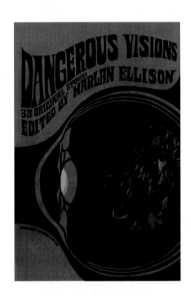

Ellison is known for introducing obscene language to the genre, which has earned him his share of detractors and supporters. It could be said that "He Has a Four-Letter Tongue and He Must Stick It Out" at his audiences, who relish his insults. Fans used to have paroxysms of laughter as he traded public insults with his good friend the late Isaac Asimov.

As an editor, he produced the watershed *Dangerous Visions* collection in 1967, in which he published 33 stories by big-name authors all writing without censorial restraints, including "A Toy for Juliette" by Robert Bloch, "Gonna Roll the Bones" by Fritz Lieber, "Lord Randy, My Son" by Joe L. Hensley, "Sex and/or Mr. Morrison" by Carol Emshwiller, "If All Men Were Brothers, Would You Let One Marry Your Sister?" by Theodore Sturgeon, and "Aye, and Gomorrah," by Samuel R. Delaney. (A second volume followed in 1972: *Again, Dangerous Visions.*) His 1968 collection was called *Love Ain't Nothing But Sex Misspelled*.

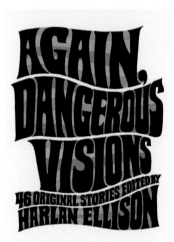

In a feat unknown to have been duplicated by any other author, he has been known to sit in a bookstore window and write a 5,000-word story from scratch.

HUGO GERNSBACK

1884–1967

Hugo Gernsback has arguably led the rest in having envisioned the most inventions-that-came-true, with Curt Siodmak being a close second. He is perhaps best known as the namesake of the Hugo Awards (presented each year at the World Science Fiction

Convention) and as *the* major pulp science fiction editor (he founded *Amazing Stories* in 1926), but he was also an accomplished inventor (and holder of around 80 patents) and the author of two significant sci-fi novels.

In April 1911, in the pages of his publication *Modern Electrics* (the premier radio magazine), 27-year-old Gernsback began serializing *Ralph 124C 41+* (read "one to foresee for one"), a romance set in the year 2660. The cover showed Ralph, one of the 10 greatest scientists of his century, using a "telephot," a person-to-person telephone/television device, which is now close to becoming a reality. (The first technical article in print using the term *television* was published by Gernsback in that same publication in December 1909!)

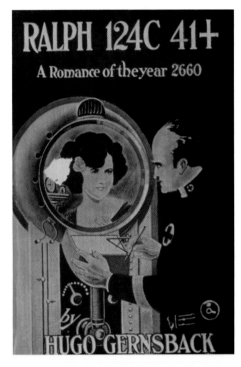

Gernsback's fiction sparked the imagination of scientists and experimenters who created libraries of microfilms projected on large screens and news printed electrolytically, without printer's ink.

In Musak, we have long had the distribution in restaurants and bars and elevators of "canned" music.

His Menograph, or thought-recorder, was the father of the modern-day lie detector. His Actinoscope: radar. Artificial silk and wool: rayon and nylon. "Glass" furniture: plastics. Luminor: fluorescent lighting.

Night-lit athletic sports, rooftop helicopter mail service, liquid fertilizer sprayed as a crop accelerator, wholesale diathermy applied to farming.... Gernsback even imagined the blood-draining of the human body and its replacement for purification—a not uncommon hospital procedure today.

Long before 2660 we will no doubt have a Gernsbackian satellite city circling the globe.

Pioneering sci-fi author Fletcher Pratt summed up Gernsback's science-fictional contribution to scientific reality: "Mr. Gernsback's educated imagination, which has preceded the normal human mind to so many things on Earth, will eventually lead us to the stars."

Talk about *Amazing*: There actually was a Russian edition of Gernsback's *Ralph 124C 41+*, but how would they know about "one to foresee"...?

ROBERT A. HEINLEIN

1907–1988

In the 1940s, Heinlein published 30 stories and three novels in John W. Campbell's *Astounding Science Fiction*, only to explode out of the pulp market altogether in the '50s. In that decade alone, he wrote an astounding 20 hardcover books, solidifying his status as one of the most-read authors in the genre. His works include *The Puppet Masters* (1951, about alien parasites), *Starship Troopers* (1959, one of his many works for juveniles, and winner of the 1960 Hugo for best novel), *Stranger in a Strange Land* (1961, with themes such as liberal sex, religious cults, and Earth–Mars relations, and winner of the 1962 Hugo for best novel), *The Moon Is a Harsh Mistress* (1966, about a computer-initiated rebellion at a penal colony on the moon, and winner of the 1967 Hugo for best novel), and *Time Enough for Love* (1973, a sequel to 1958's *Methuselah's Children*). Heinlein was the guest of honor at three World Science Fiction Conventions (and the only one ever to be booed, for praising war as an ennobling necessity).

In his 1942 short novel *Waldo*, Heinlein wrote of the Synchronous Reduplicating Pantograph, which permitted one to place his or her hands in gloves and manipulate objects as though one's hands were actually on them. The device is now a fundamental tool in many virtual reality applications, and is often aptly referred to as . . . a waldo!

Heinlein conceptualized the "future history," a literary device that has been used by many subsequent sci-fi writers. Future histories are essentially time lines of years or eras to come: Readers use them to place particular stories by a given writer into the correct historical context. According to Heinlein's future history, 20th-century man is still in his childhood or adolescence; it won't be until the early 22nd century that humankind matures into what will be the first truly human civilization.

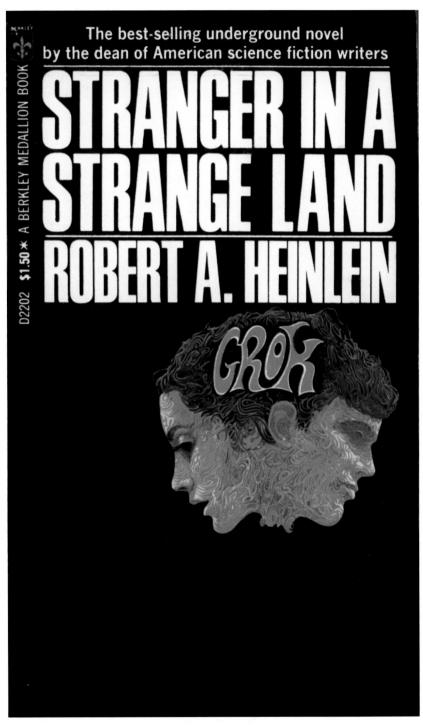

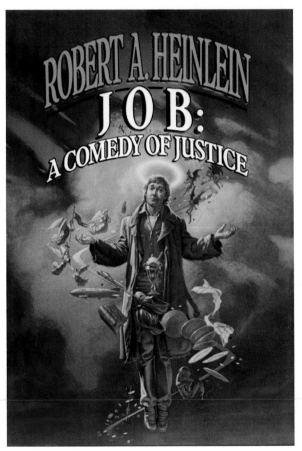

ALDOUS HUXLEY

1894-1963

Huxley was many things—social critic, playwright, university lecturer, novelist—but he was not primarily a science fiction writer. However, four of his works had such significant impact on the field that his name invariably surfaces among serious sci-fi aficionados. *Brave New World* (1933) is, of course, his world-famous futuristic dystopia.

After Many a Summer Dies the Swan (1939) is about aging and immortality, among other things, and features a 200-year-old couple (that has grown more apelike and less human). *Ape and Essence* (1948) is a postnuclear holocaust novel that influenced Nevil Shute's *On the Beach* (1957) and Walter Miller's classic *A Canticle for Leibowitz* (a 1961 Hugo Award winner). And *Island* (1962) is about a Utopian society.

In *Brave New World*, Huxley predicted a drug called soma. In the mid-'50s, a tranquilizing drug called Miltown took an unsuspecting public, especially individuals in entertainment, by storm. Everybody was popping pills to quiet their nerves and keep themselves in equilibrium. Paul Coates, a popular TV personality of the time, wanted to devote a segment of his show to these brand-new drugs. (A rival brand was actually named Soma.) Coates called me in the hopes that I could put him in touch with Huxley, who I knew was off to Washington to lecture on his new nonfiction book, *Brave New World Revisited*. Coates was very disappointed to hear that Huxley was unavailable, but just off the tip of my tongue I began to reel off sci-fi stories that described drugs with properties similar to soma. Chu-chu gum was one in David Keller's 1948 story, "The Abyss"; although it was not a drug, "The Emotion Gas" by a little-known sci-fi pulp writer and "The Truth Gas" by famous-in-his-day Edmond Hamilton had similar effects. On and on I went, so impressing the TV journalist that the next thing I knew I was on the air substituting for Aldous Huxley!

Asked by Coates what warning was implied in the predictions of David Keller, Arthur K. Barnes ("The Emotion Solution"), and Evan Hunter ("Malice in Wonderland"), I replied: "Go slow. Approach the use of tranquility drugs with . . . tranquility. Do we want willpower replaced by pill power? Anxiety may be akin to ambition, and if human emotions are canceled out of the equation of life we may end up automatons, Capekian robots feeling neither grief nor joy nor fear nor love nor any of the human emotions."

DAVID H. KELLER

1880-1966

Keller is a rare breed in the world of science fiction writers, for he wasn't even published until he was almost 50 years old. The arrival of the pulps in the late '20s provided a vehicle for his stories, which he'd been writing and sharing with friends and family for years simply for the love of it all. In the '30s, he published more than 50 stories, which were referred to by editors and fans as "Kelleryarns," though some clearly belonged to the horror and fantasy genres.

Keller was born in 1880 in Monroe County, Pennsylvania. He had a sister several years older on whom his mother lavished all her love and attention. Little David got the message, and gave one of his own: IF YOU DON'T CARE FOR ME, I DON'T CARE FOR YOU. He closed his ears to any questions or comments directed toward him; instead he created a language all his own, which he taught to his sister. "I was sent home from kindergarten," he told me, "because I didn't understand anything that was being said to me." Teachers took him to be the village idiot. Then, when his sister was eight, she died, leaving little David incommunicado with the world. Ultimately, he would learn English, but he always dreamed in his personal language, and it influenced his writing.

The themes of language and children permeate some of Keller's work; in fact, Keller was noted for having more babies per square paragraph than any other science fiction author of his day ("Unto Us a Child Is Born," "The Psychophonic Nurse," "The Lost Language"). Readers sometimes feel in reading his work that it has been translated not from, let's say, French or German or any known language, but from something unknown—as indeed it was, as he revealed in "The Lost Language."

Before his late-life career as a writer, Keller was a physician, professor, and psychoanalyst: His professional perspectives, as well as his personal struggles, often inform his narrative voices.

Although known in some circles for his huge ego (he would offer others 50 cents to listen to him brag about himself for a half hour), he was the most altruistic science fiction author ever born when it came to giving away his stories for free to young fanzine editors.

HENRY KUTTNER and C. L. MOORE

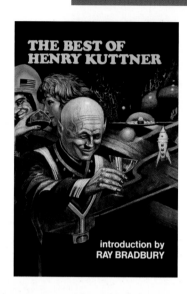

HK 1915-1958
CLM 1911-1987

When the editor of *Weird Tales*, Farnsworth Wright, received C. L. Moore's manuscript for "Shambleau," he declared to his office staff, "This is the finest story we've ever received." It was published in the November 1933 issue, and readership appreciation was overwhelming.

Henry Kuttner, another contributor to *Weird* (it published "The Graveyard Rats" in 1936), wrote a fan letter to "Mr. C. L. Moore." Moore responded and he learned of her female identity; he met her and it was love at first sight. The two were married in 1940, and they became professional collaborators until Kuttner's death in 1958.

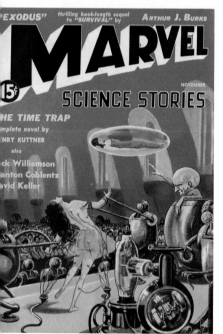

They are two of the most underappreciated figures in the world of science fiction. Perhaps this can be attributed to the fact that much of their work is in the fantasy/adventure mode—Kuttner was frequently published in *Startling Stories* and *Thrilling Adventures*—but eventually he (they) became a mainstay at *Astounding Science Fiction*. Because they both had a penchant for pen names, and because they wrote almost everything together, one can never be sure if one is reading one of her stories or one of his—chances are they're all true collaborations.

I suspect that they've also been overlooked by many critics and fans because they never produced a classic novel that was a best-selling sensation, as did contemporaries such as Asimov, Heinlein, or Orwell, although their collaborative novel *Fury* (1950; also known as *Destination Infinity*) is excellent science fiction. But they were masters of the short form; their stories are available today in numerous collections (some attributed to Kuttner, such as *Robots Have No Tails*, and some attributed to Moore, such as *Northwest of Earth*).

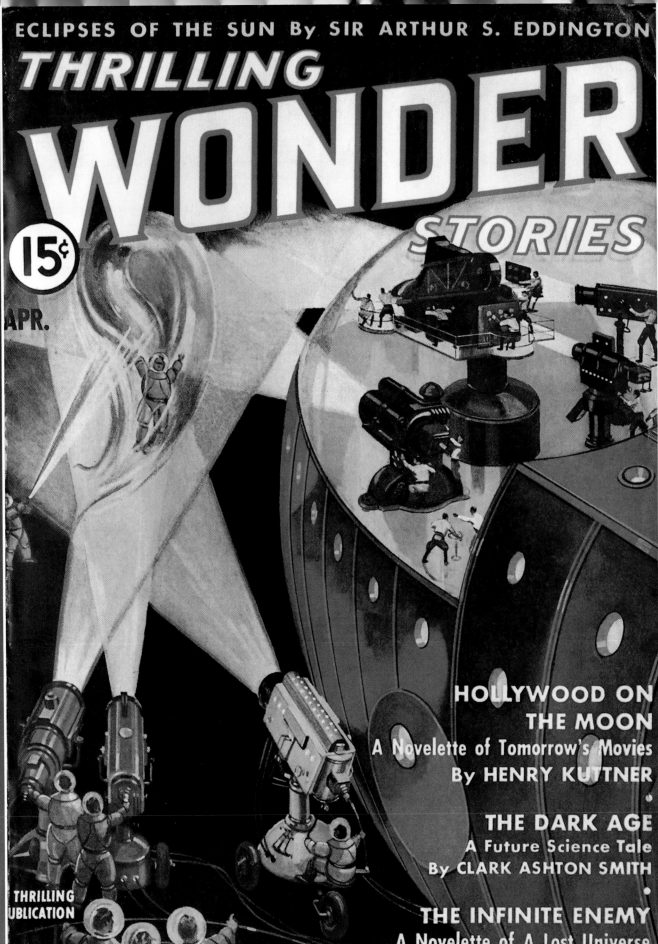

ECLIPSES OF THE SUN By SIR ARTHUR S. EDDINGTON

THRILLING
WONDER
STORIES

15¢

APR.

HOLLYWOOD ON
THE MOON
A Novelette of Tomorrow's Movies
By HENRY KUTTNER

THE DARK AGE
A Future Science Tale
By CLARK ASHTON SMITH

THE INFINITE ENEMY
A Novelette of A Lost Universe
By JACK WILLIAMSON

THRILLING
PUBLICATION

MURRAY LEINSTER

1896–1975

Leinster, often referred to as the Dean of Science Fiction, had his first story published in *Argosy* in 1919. The story was "The Runaway Skyscraper," and it came to the attention of science fiction readers when reprinted in the third issue of *Amazing Stories* in June 1926. It bears one of the most memorable and often-quoted lines in the history of science fiction: "The whole thing started when the clock on the Metropolitan Tower began to run backward."

Leinster did not stop writing until 1970, so his body of work is huge. His sci-fi classic is considered to be "First Contact" (1945), in which Earth astronauts meet alien astronauts in deep space; both have trouble determining whether the intentions of the other are friendly or militant.

Among his other classics are "The Mad Planet" (1920), which evolved into the novel *The Forgotten Planet* (1954), and "Sidewise in Time" (1934), in which Leinster explores the possibility of a parallel universe.

ABRAHAM MERRITT

1884–1943

Merritt's first job was as a newspaper reporter in Philadelphia at which he was assigned all the seamy stories—everything from crimes to catastrophes. Considered the best man to cover executions (!), he confessed that the assignments sickened him. In 1937, he became editor-in-chief of the *American Weekly*, the Hearst Sunday newspaper supplement featuring "true" stories of guillotined heads speaking after decapitation, native voodoo, ghosts, sunken treasures, Atlantis, inexplicable events, terrifying experiences—everything but flying saucers (which hadn't arrived yet). I gloried in

Merritt's section as a kid, asking my maternal grandfather on Sundays for "the terrible part" of the paper.

His sci-fi classics include *The Moon Pool* (1919) and its lesser sequel, *The Metal Monster* (1920). His sci-fi–oriented novel *Burn, Witch, Burn!* reached the silver screen as Tod Browning's *The Devil Doll* in 1936, costarring Lionel Barrymore as the people-shrinking scientist and Maureen O'Sullivan as his daughter.

BOB OLSEN

1884-1956

Olsen's first contribution to *Amazing Stories* was 1927's "The Four Dimensional Roller Press," which was followed by five more very popular fourth-dimension stories. But he is probably more well-remembered as the ant's best friend: One could easily call him the best of the "sci-ants" fiction writers. He tenderly cultivated them in his backyard in Beverly Hills. "They're my children," he once told me. He shared information about his formicary inhabitants in tales such as "The Ant with a Human Soul" (1932) and "Peril Among the Drivers" (1934).

In 1931, a short-lived sci-fi magazine appeared titled *Miracle, Science and Fantasy Stories* (it was notable for introducing the artist Elliott Dold Jr.). In its second and final number, it advertised a sensational work scheduled for issue No. 3. That story was the aforementioned "Ant with a Human Soul." When the manuscript was accepted for publication, the acceptance letter was wired to Olsen and read aloud by a Western Union lady over the phone. It read OFFER $200 FOR ANT WITH A HUMAN SOUL. Not realizing it was the title of a novel, she blurted, "Excuse me, sir, I've heard of trained fleas in circuses, but is that possible—an ant with a human soul?!"

There never was a third issue of *Miracle, Science and Fantasy Stories*; the tale was first published in 1932 in *Amazing Stories Quarterly*.

GEORGE ORWELL

1903–1950

It is one thing to call a book one of the best in its genre; it is quite another to call it one of the best in *any* genre. But so it is with Orwell's *Nineteen Eighty-Four*.

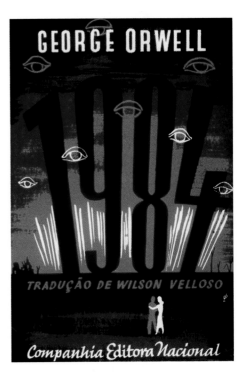

The book had great impact upon its release in 1949 for two reasons. First, its predecessor, *Animal Farm* (Orwell's fifth novel), had been his first significant success, so this book was a highly anticipated follow-up. Second, and more important, the Holocaust was a fresh memory. Brainwashing, nationalism, A-bombs, unconscionable acts by an unconscionable totalitarian government were not out of the realm of possibility—in fact, it was all pretty recent history.

The tale is Orwell's statement on the sacred nature of human liberty. Set in a post–World War III society, the story chronicles the complete dehumanization of Winston Smith by the Party in power, which employs him in its Ministry of Truth, where he "translates" (rewrites) history and current events into the Party's language, Newspeak. In a society in which feelings are outlawed, Smith makes the criminal mistake of falling in love. And he pays the price.

Orwell is not generally thought of as a sci-fi writer; *Animal Farm* is certainly fantasy with its talking pigs and cows, rather than science fiction. But *Nineteen Eighty-Four* set the standard for sci-fi dystopias, a benchmark that one could argue has never been surpassed.

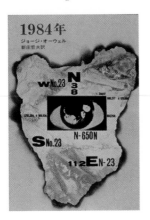

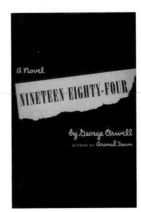

ERIC FRANK RUSSELL

1905-1978

Russell first came into contact with science fiction fandom in the mid-'30s as a member of the British Interplanetary Society. His "Sinister Barrier," influenced by Charles Fort, of whose work he was an ardent admirer, was the lead story in the first issue of *Unknown* (1939), editor John W. Campbell Jr.'s companion to *Astounding*.

"Dreadful Sanctuary," serialized in *Astounding* in 1948, was another instant hit, and first set me to wondering if Earth isn't indeed the insane asylum of the universe.

"Allamagoosa" won the 1955 Hugo Award for best short story.

John Campbell said in 1968 that Russell was his favorite science fiction author, high praise indeed from the editor who introduced and championed many a sci-fi pioneer.

ALADRA SEPTAMA

UNKNOWN

Although less than a handful of the dwindling legion of pioneer sci-fi readers will remember Septama, he produced six space operas in a two-year period, including *The Cry from the Ether* (an unforgettable title if there ever was one), *Tani of Ekkis*, and *Dragons of Space*. Aladra Septama was the pen name of a San Francisco lawyer, Judson W. Reeves. Perhaps I remember him because he took a young, starstruck boy named Forry Ackerman to lunch and gave him an amazing stack of *Amazing Stories* 1926 back issues!

THEODORE STURGEON

1918-1985

Sturgeon was more sexually oriented in his science fiction than most authors. But his was not sleazy sex or sex for sensationalism; rather, Sturgeon explored sex as an integral part of the human psyche. He has many classic stories, including "Ether Breather" (1939), "Microcosmic God" (1941), "Bianca's Hands" (1947), "Thunder and Roses" (1947), "The Sex Opposite" (1952), a tale of two homosexual aliens in "The World Well Lost" (1953), "The Cosmic Rape" (1958), the hermaphroditic "Venus Plus X" (1961), and the incest tale "If All Men Were Brothers, Would You Let One Marry Your Sister?" (1967). The novel *More Than Human* (1953) is classic Sturgeon, mixing love and sex and the paranormal.

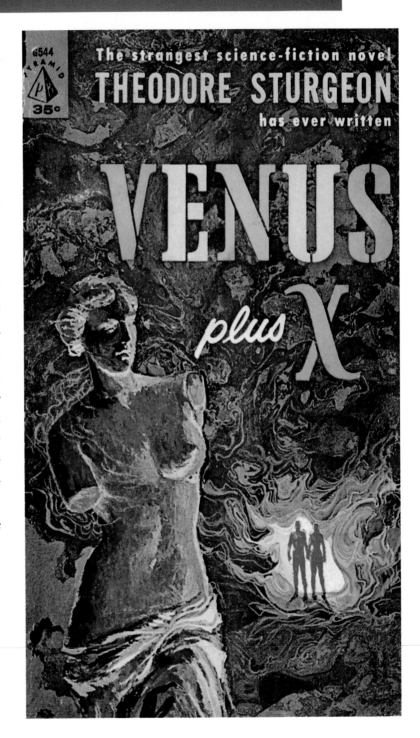

GARRETT PUTNAM SERVISS

1851–1929

His biographer, Everett F. Bleiler, refers to Serviss as "one of the most important science fiction novelists in America before World War I," even though his sci-fi output was limited to half a dozen titles, including *Edison's Conquest of Mars* (1898); *The Moon Metal* (1900); *A Columbus of Space* (1909), about the first trip to Venus (and dedicated to Jules Verne); and *The Second Deluge* (1911).

With *Edison's Conquest*, he created the "edisonade," a sci-fi rendering of an inventor who saves the country, or the universe, with some new technology. (The subgenre was perfected by E. E. Smith in 1928's *The Skylark of Space*.) Serviss died in 1929, but lived to see *Moon Metal*, *Columbus*, and *Deluge* reprinted in *Amazing Stories* and *Amazing Stories Quarterly*.

'Standing on the steps . . . was a creature shaped like a man, but more savage than a gorilla."

[Page 47.]

M. P. SHIEL

1865-1947

Shiel was a most unusual writer. Today, many would consider this British author an outright racist, but in the context of his time, he was simply a nationalist who chronicled future wars with great detail and imagination—who cared if the enemies were always the Chinese, Japanese, or Jews, and the victors the Brits?

The Purple Cloud (1901) is one of his few works that is still known and appreciated by sci-fi readers. When his protagonist completes his solo trek to the North Pole, he is unaware that a purple volcanic gas has destroyed the rest of the human race—save for one lone female. His dilemma upon discovering the girl: Eat her or love her?

That novel was highly regarded by H. G. Wells and given a new life when reprinted in 1949 in the pulp *Famous Fantastic Mysteries*. Archivist Everett F. Bleiler considers him "the novelistic daredevil who plotted like Cecil B. DeMille—who smashed mankind in purple prose, drowned 10 million in the Maelstrom…and pulled diamonds out of the sky."

CLIFFORD D. SIMAK

1904-1988

Simak is an anomaly in the world of science fiction writers. Though he began writing in the '30s when sci-fi writing was heavily influenced by world wars and explored the combination of man's dark nature and the perils of technology, Simak became the genre's resident optimist. Most of his works were published in the '60s and '70s, when the heretofore unspoken evils of racism and sexual repression were given loud voice by journalists, academics, and fiction writers; and yet Simak had a cheery disposition. His work is filled with all the sci-fi staples: extraterrestrials, robots, time machines, parallel universes, mystical fantasy characters with magic powers. But instead of annihilating the enemy aliens or outsmarting the neighborhood dinosaurs, Simak's Earthlings make peace with them and learn to coexist.

Simak won Hugo Awards in 1959 and 1964 for "The Big Front Yard" and *Way Station*, respectively. He wrote until his death in 1988.

CURT SIODMAK

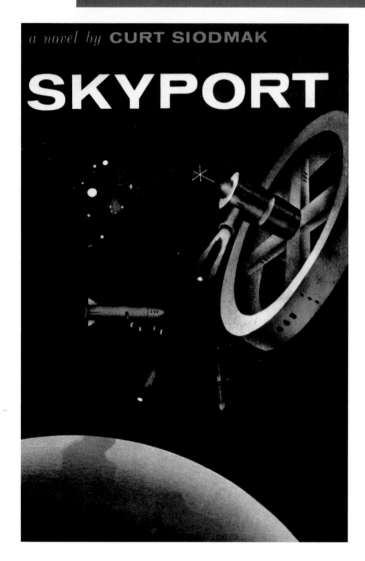

a novel by **CURT SIODMAK**

SKYPORT

1902-

Curt Siodmak is a novelist, short-story writer, screenwriter, and a sometimes-director. His most popular novel is *Donovan's Brain*, which Hollywood presented three times (1944's *The Lady and the Monster*, 1953's *Donovan's Brain*, and 1962's *The Brain*). Business tycoon and criminal Donovan dies in a plane crash, but his brain is saved by researcher Patrick Cory, who treats it with chemicals to keep it alive. It not only lives on; it assumes telepathic powers and eventually controls Cory. Disaster ensues.

But Siodmak is so much more than *Donovan's Brain*, despite its enduring popularity. Siodmak was a sci-fi prophet in his own right. His 1932 scientifilm *F. P. 1 Antwortet Nicht (F. P. 1 Doesn't Answer)* was about a not-yet-invented Floating Platform of steel and glass in the mid-Atlantic. Such a platform would provide the only means for airplanes, then incapable of flying at supersonic speeds, to cross the ocean. (In the same vein, 1937's *Non-Stop New York* was about trans-Atlantic jet travel.) And in his 1954 film, *Riders to the Stars*, a massive, menacing meteor from the void is headed on a disastrous collision course with Earth. Siodmak's solution to such a calamity was devised 43 years earlier than that depicted in the 1997 NBC miniseries *Asteroid*.

OLAF STAPLEDON

1886–1950

When one thinks of Stapledon, one thinks of scope. His future history takes readers 200 billion years hence. Stapledon keeps the nomenclature simple in his future history (no Neanderthals and Cro-Magnons here): The Second Men rise somewhere around A.D. 10,000,000, to be followed by the Third Men, the Fourth Men, and so on, until the 18th (or Last) Men in the year 2,000,000,000. His first work, the classic *Last and First Men* (1930), describes mankind's history on Earth, Mars, and Neptune. I personally prefer 1932's lesser known *Last Men in London,* and 1944's *Sirius,* named for the genetically altered dog with human intelligence that falls deeply in love with the young woman with whom he's been raised.

According to sci-fi-fan-turned-historian Sam Moskowitz, Stapledon's was "the most titanic imagination ever brought to science fiction."

JOHN TAINE

1883-1960

Between 1924 and 1955, a master mathematician named Eric Temple Bell published 13 novels under the pseudonym John Taine. His fiction was science to the core—technological mishaps, biological oddities, natural disasters, ethical dilemmas—but his stories unfolded like mysteries (1924's *The Purple Sapphire* and 1952's *The Crystal Horde*) and were influenced by world events (1954's *G.O.G. 666* revolves around a suspicious Soviet experiment).

Taine's 1928 novel, *Green Fire: The Story of the Terrible Days in the Summer of 1990*, about an atomic chain reaction threatening Earth's destruction, was produced in the early '30s on Broadway as a play.

Taine survived the San Francisco earthquake of 1906 and 25 years later incorporated memories of it into his *Wonder Stories* serial, "The Time Stream," which is certainly a time-travel classic. (It was finally published as a novel in 1946.)

A. E. VAN VOGT

1912–

A. E. van Vogt was a major figure in the 1940s—the Golden Age of Science Fiction. His stories appeared regularly in the pulps, particularly *Astounding Science Fiction*. Later on, van Vogt would combine short stories to build novels. For example, his 1939 stories "Black Destroyer" and "Discord in Scarlet," plus 1943's "M33 in Andromeda" and 1950's "War of Nerves," became the 1950 novel *The Voyage of the Space Beagle*. Likewise, three early '40s stories—"The Great Engine," "The Changeling," and "The Beast"—became the 1963 novel *The Beast*. Both are masterworks.

His other classics include *Slan* (1946), *The Weapon Makers* (1947), *The World of Null-A* (1956), and *Quest for the Future* (1970).

He is known for writing in 800-word blocks, a technique devised to keep each page fresh and full of suspense, to maintain a fast rhythm, to hook the reader and not let go. Some critics have suggested that this device presented character inconsistencies and plot implausibilities, but van Vogt devotees remain impressed with his fantastic imagination and enjoy being transported to places that most other writers could not even venture.

I served as editor of his collection *Science Fiction Monsters* (1965) and had the privilege of collaborating with him on (the totally inconsequential) "Laugh, Clone, Laugh," my personal spoof of the era of New Wave, which I considered errant nonsense.

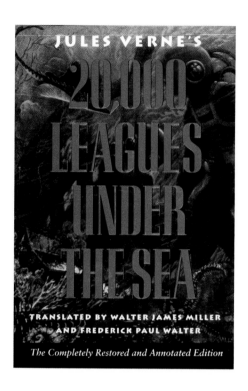

JULES VERNE

1828-1905

"He insisted on making everything plausible and his gift for prophecy was based on a firm scientific foundation."

—Donald H. Tuck, *The Encyclopedia of Science Fiction and Fantasy*

When the modern submarine—electrically motored and designed to stay underwater indefinitely—was invented and a patent applied for, it was denied because Verne had so incredibly described its workings in *Twenty Thousand Leagues Under the Sea* (1870).

Deeply inspired by the stories of Edgar Allan Poe, Verne (often referred to as the Father of Science Fiction) has in turn inspired 20th-century authors; Ray Bradbury, in particular, has acknowledged Verne as a major influence on his work. Among his major works are *A Journey to the Center of the Earth* (1864), *From the Earth to the Moon* (1865; on which the Méliès film *A Trip to the Moon* is loosely based), *Twenty Thousand Leagues*, and the non–science fiction *Around the World in Eighty Days* (1873); however, Verne published dozens of titles and all of the available anthologies are worth any reader's while.

A note of interest: Verne's *Off on a Comet* (1877), in which protagonist Hector Servadac and his servant are scooped up by a comet and given a tour of this solar system, was the inspiration for Frank R. Paul's cover on the first issue of *Amazing Stories* in April 1926.

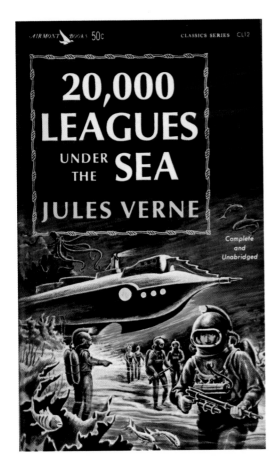

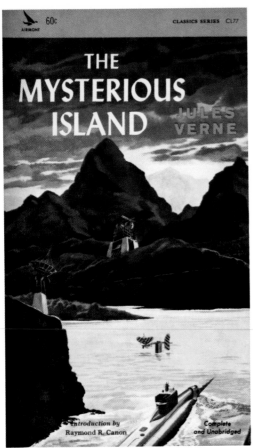

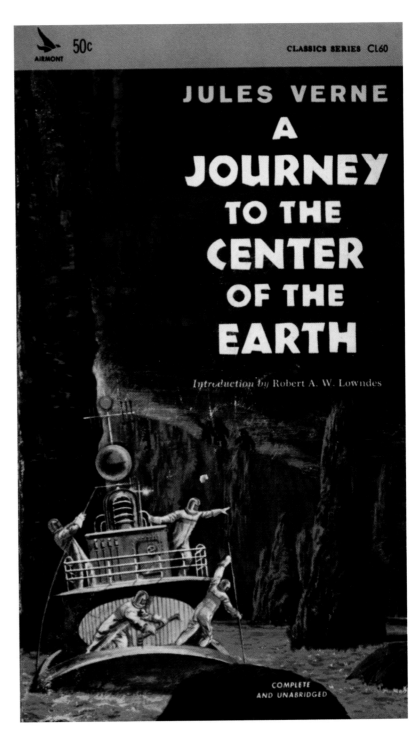

STANLEY GRAUMAN WEINBAUM

1902-1935

On a hot summer day in 1934, I was underneath an umbrella on the beach at Ocean Park, my toes curled in the sand in excitement as I read "A Martian Odyssey" by a new author I had never heard of before. I did not know then that the story, published in *Wonder Stories,* would one day be voted the second most popular science fiction story of all time by the Science Fiction Writers of America.

Weinbaum was the first sci-fi author to break out of the mold of monstrous interplanetary aliens—popularized by H. G. Wells, Edmond Hamilton, Ray Cummings, Arthur J. Burks, and other early sci-fi practitioners—and present a Martian (Tweel, an endearing birdlike being) as a sympathetic creature. "A Martian Odyssey" was followed by a sequel, "The Valley of Dreams," and in the ensuing 17 months until his untimely death of cancer of the throat in 1935, he continued to entertain the sci-fi audience of the day and influence fellow authors such as Arthur K. Barnes and Eric Frank Russell. *Dawn of Flame* (1939) is a commemorative collection of short stories that is a valuable collector's item.

In addition to his "interplanetaryarns" ("The Red Peri" was his first space opera), he told wonder stories of time travel, medical miracles, future America, and one of my favorite superman novels of all time, *The New Adam* (1939). His "The Adaptive Element" (1935), published under the pseudonym of John Jessel, was filmed as *She-Devil* (1957).

S. FOWLER WRIGHT

1874-1965

Like David H. Keller, Wright was a late bloomer; he was in his 50s when his first novel, *The Amphibians: A Romance of 500,000 Years Hence,* was published in 1925.

In 1927, *Deluge* brought him world renown. In it, he drowned nearly all of Great Britain. *Deluge* had a sequel, *Dawn,* and the two were combined into the 1933 RKO film adaptation, also called *Deluge,* in which New York City suffers an earthquake and a tidal wave in quick succession. The special effects were exceptional.

The World Below (1929) is one of the four or five greatest science fiction novels ever published. In this time-travel tale, Wright brings readers hundreds of thousands of years into the future to see how far we've "progressed"—man still has a frightening lack of regard for other living things.

I was Wright's literary agent for a while in the 1950s, and at one point he gave me an ultimatum: If I didn't want to lose him as a client, I had one year to prove myself with a major sale. So, naturally, I thought it was time to bring *The World Below* back into print in a pocketbook edition, and I approached my friend, longtime-fan-turned-pro-publisher Don Wollheim. And to my astonishment and disbelief, he turned it down! This was a book that made the top five in a sci-fi readers poll a few years earlier. I tried to persuade Wollheim that it would be a cinch to find some great quotes for the back cover from powerful names in the field, and that if we graced the cover with a naked female amphibian heroine and a frog-man and a bat-man, he'd have a surefire seller. But he said readers didn't recognize the name S. Fowler Wright anymore. Period. End of story. Instead, he published all kinds of new-school hack writers and passed on a classic.

I lost Wright as a client and I never really got over the blow, but I also have never stopped believing in *The World Below.*

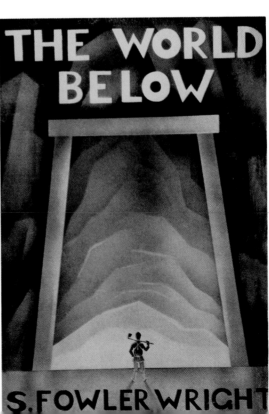

H. G. WELLS

1866-1946

Film director-producer Alexander Korda shows H. G. Wells his preparations for *Things to Come* (1936).

Wells's major sci-fi novels include *The Time Machine* (1895), *The Island of Doctor Moreau* (1896), *The Invisible Man* (1897), *The War of the Worlds* (1898), *The First Men in the Moon* (1901), and *The Shape of Things to Come* (1933); there are dozens of classic Wells short stories as well. Twenty-six of his works were serialized in *Amazing Stories* by editor Hugo Gernsback during its first four years of publication.

In the second edition of *Twentieth-Century Science-Fiction Writers* (St. James Press, 1986), Wells is given his due as a prophet: "Wells foresaw tank warfare in 1903 ("The Land Ironclads"), massive bombardment of cities by aircraft in 1908 (*The War in the Air*), and atomic bombs in 1914 (*The World Set Free*)."

Hollywood has produced mixed results of Wells's work. He lived to see *Island of Lost Souls* (1932), based on his *Doctor Moreau* novel, but was irked by the script's overexaggerated, tyrannical take on Moreau's character. *The Invisible Man* (1933), directed by James Whale just two years after his classic *Frankenstein*, was faithful to the novel and Claude Rains was wonderful, but a number of "sequels," culminating in *Abbott and Costello Meet the Invisible Man* (1951), have nothing whatsoever to do with Wells. Raymond Massey and Ralph Richardson starred in *Things to Come* (1936), based on the novel *The Shape of Things to Come*, and this film holds up well. It takes us from World War II in 1940 (Wells was only off by a few years) to a faux Utopia in 2036 in which peace gas has abolished both war and human individuality.

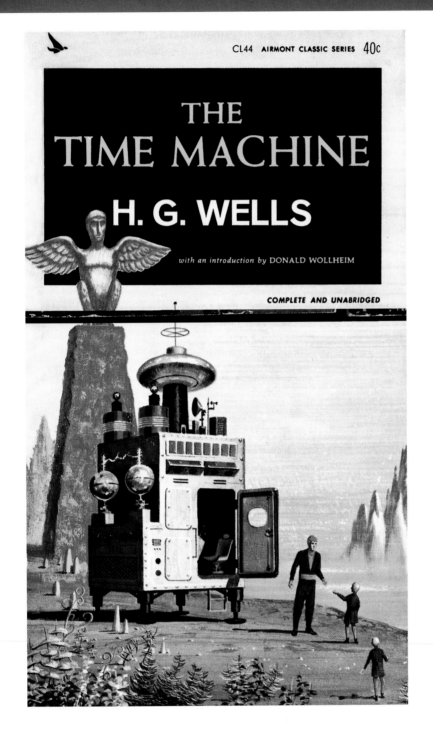

FIRST MEN IN THE MOON

H. G. WELLS

Wells published many non–science fiction and non-fiction works, and his later works are not considered great by many an annoying critic or connoisseur, but no one can argue that he produced more enduring, still-in-print, still-read classics in a 10-year period than most writers in any genre do in a lifetime.

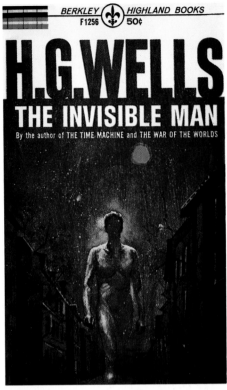

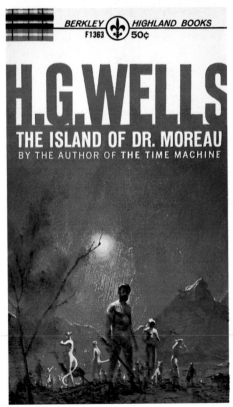

EVERYDAY
Science and Mechanics

Sept.

HUGO GERNSBACK
Editor

A GERNSBACK PUBLICATION

25 Cents
Canada 30¢

100 YEARS HENCE

See Page 910

LATEST INVENTIONS, AERO-MECHANICS, SHOP KINKS, TELEVISION, EXPERIMENTS
FORMULAS, CHEMISTRY, WOOD AND METAL CRAFTS; RADIO KINKS

CHAPTER THREE

Amazing! Astounding! Incredible!

Pulp Science Fiction

The word *pulp* refers to the cheap quality of the paper used in old magazines, although to many it also connotes the sensational nature of the material therein. One thinks of cheap romance stories or gossip publications when one hears *pulp*, not literature. But science fiction is definitely literature, and many of America's greatest writers were published in the pulps.

Amazing Stories
THE GOLDEN YEARS

"EXTRAVAGANT FICTION TODAY . . . COLD FACT TOMORROW." That was what editor/publisher Hugo Gernsback promised when the April 1926 *Amazing Stories* appeared on the newsstands. In addition to Verne's "Off on a Comet," H. G. Wells was represented with "The New Accelerator," Edgar Allan Poe with "The Facts in the Case of M. Valdemar," George Allen England with "The Thing from—Outside," Austin Hall with "The Man Who Saved the Earth," and a talented teenager named G. Peyton Wertenbaker with "The Man from the Atom." Wertenbaker was later in life to be known as mainstream author Green Peyton. A heady mixture for, mainly, young men of America. Years later I learned that the cover by the Master, Frank R. Paul, was only a preliminary painting and was not intended to be the final product (see page 30). Nevertheless, it served its market well.

For its first few years, of necessity, *Amazing Stories* depended on reprints by famous authors, as there were very few newcomers to the field. The third issue reintroduced

Futuristic visions were a staple on the pulp covers of the early '30s, as on this cover painted by Frank R. Paul for the September 1932 issue of *Everyday Science and Mechanics*—a magazine full of lavishly illustrated articles about inventions.

December 1926

Murray Leinster with what was to become a classic, "The Runaway Skyscraper," whose opening line has been memorized and repeated ad infinitum in the history of science fiction: "The whole thing started when the clock on the Metropolitan Tower began to run backward."

The fourth issue is significant because it gave the American audience its first taste of German/Jewish author Curt Siodmak with "The Eggs from Lake Tanganyika." Siodmak is known today for *Donovan's Brain* (filmed three times) and its two sequels, and scripts for scores of sci-fi films, including *F. P. 1* (1932), *Transatlantic Tunnel* (1935), *Frankenstein Meets the Wolf Man* (1943), and *Riders to the Stars* (1954).

The August issue of *Amazing Stories* introduced the current audience to *A Columbus of Space,* a novel first published in 1909 by Professor Garrett P. Serviss and still quite Servissable in 1926. The next few issues featured authors like fantasist A. Merritt (with "The Face in the Abyss") and A. Hyatt Verrill ("Beyond the Pole").

The December 1926 featured a $500 prize contest (a fortune in the days of penny postcards and two-cent stamps) for the best story based on the Frank R. Paul cover. Of 360 submissions, the winner was "The Visitation" by Cyril G. Wates of Canada, who went on to publish three stories in later issues. Second prize went to "The Electronic Wall" by George R. Fox (who was never to be heard from again). Third prize went to "The Fate of the Poseidonia," and was significant in that it introduced a woman writer, Clare Winger Harris, to the pages of *Amazing Stories*. She become a regular contributor: Her "Miracle of the Lily" is regarded as a classic, as is a story she coauthored with Miles J. Breuer called "A Baby on Neptune."

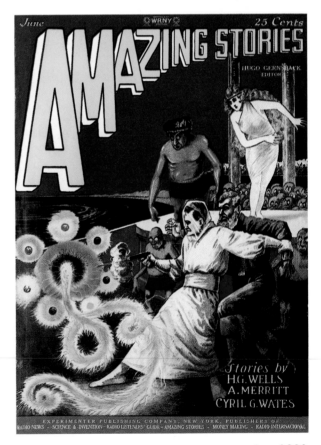

June 1928

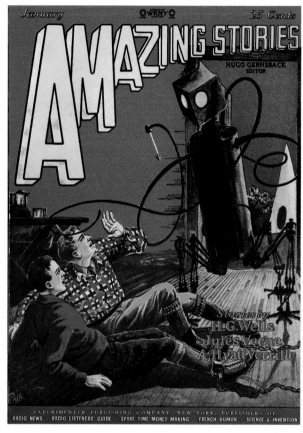 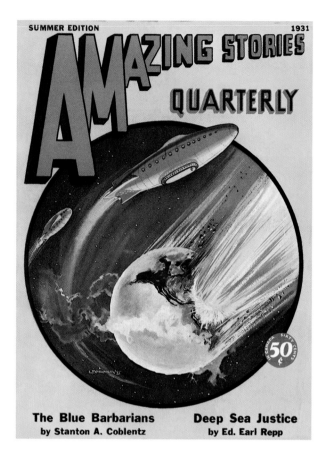

Left, January 1928; right, Summer 1931

The March 1927 issue featured a reprint of a seven-year-old story, "The Green Splotches," by T. S. Stribling, who went on to win the 1933 Pulitzer Prize for fiction for *The Store*. Editor Gernsback alerted his readers: "If any one were to ask us for a perfect example of the scientifiction story, we would perhaps unhesitantly say 'The Green Splotches.' Here is a story that mixes science with fiction to the nth degree." A. Merritt also was featured with "The People of the Pit" and Edgar Rice Burroughs with "The Land That Time Forgot." The June 1927 edition is a collectors' item because of its installment of Merritt's legendary novel, *The Moon Pool*. Another Frank R. Paul illustration graced the cover.

Under Gernsback, the successful sister publication *Amazing Stories Annual* (later *Amazing Stories Quarterly*) was launched in 1928. Gernsback left *Amazing* (to found *Science Wonder Stories* (see page 118), and was succeeded by Arthur Lynch in mid-1929, but Lynch's tenure lasted only five issues. T. O'Conor Sloane was the *Amazing* editor from November 1929 to April 1938, during which time the magazine became a perennial bore. Sloane actually declared in print that no rocket would ever reach the moon—sacrilege for a sci-fi editor.

THE PALMER YEARS

With the June 1938 issue, *Amazing Stories* underwent a sea change. An actual pioneering fan—Raymond A. Palmer—became editor, and he was on a mission to up the circulation and appeal to a more mainstream audience. "Insofar as the basic subject matter is founded upon scientific research," wrote Palmer in the Observatory by the Editor column, "it will be essentially a true story magazine although thrilling tenseness of adventure and romance will still form a part of the many features yet to come."

The front cover, reprinted here, was a novelty: Instead of a vibrantly colored illustration, Palmer chose a posed photograph of a spaceman with a fainted heroine over one arm. (Looking at it 60 years later, it still looks pretty good to me.) Of the back cover (see pages 112–113), he wrote:

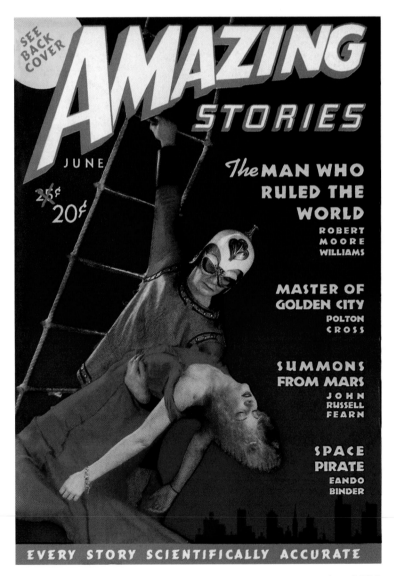

June 1938

18 DAYS TO
THE MOON

723 YEARS
TO NEPTUNE

462 YEARS
TO URANUS

202 YEARS
TO SATURN

125 YEARS
TO JUPITER

24 YEARS
TO SUN

This Amazing

Our whirling universe is much too vast to illustrate in correct
proportions. It would require a sheet 100 miles long! Ignoring
relative proportions, this Illustrated Chart visualizes the tremendous

ILLUSTRATION BY HAROLD W. MC CAULEY

648 MILLION YEARS TO NEAREST STAR   36 YEARS TO MARS   24 YEARS TO VENUS   24 YEARS TO MERCURY   957 YEARS TO PLUTO

Universe

distances between our Earth and its nearest neighbors. Travelling
in the world's fastest airplane (440) miles per hour it takes 24 years
to reach Venus; 957 years to Pluto! Further details on page 107.

We think that you will get a huge kick out of [it]. We believe that it will help you to realize what distance really means in this universe of ours. Zeros running all over the page and terms such as "light years" are almost impossible for our meagre consciousness to grasp.

The interior art was inferior but fans were catered to with bios of the authors and a free Correspondence Corner, in which fans with particular interests—e.g., astronomy or chemistry—could list their addresses and get pen pals.

The April 1939 issue of *Amazing* was selected to be buried in the time capsule at the New York World's Fair grounds, to be dug up in the year 2039—I saw it happen. (Will anyone remember when the year rolls round or know where to locate it?)

With the July 1940 issue, Ray Palmer began to use Frank R. Paul's artwork in the interior once again, and he inaugurated a series of back covers by the Master, for which he shall forever remain blessed. The first (see page 116) featured barrel-chested, big-eared, antennaed Martians—which had been the popular concept since the middle of the 1920s—as they are regarding a statue of an Earthman constructed from their best scientific theories. As Planet 3 (Earth) is three-quarters water, it is reasonable for them to assume that a human would be quasi-amphibian. Due to the abundant food he would be a "fat, contented creature, with a large body, bullet-head, short legs, and webbed hands and feet.... [W]e of Mars can

July 1940

April 1939

AS MARS SEES US

A Martian reconstruction of the Earthman, deduced from what he can discover of our world by observation and analysis, might very logically be such a creature as is shown here. (For complete explanation see page 144.)

well be jealous of Earth and its inhabitants." Paul's back cover depiction of the Earthman is a scream. In the lower left-hand corner, of no particular significance to the overall painting, is what appears to be in the hands of a Martian a painting of the Earth as viewed from space. Until the late '60s, when we actually saw our planet from space, it had always been depicted in green. *Paul painted it blue!*

In January 1942, the price of *Amazing* went up a nickel but the publication virtually doubled in size.

The July 1943 cover was by McCauley and is memorable because it featured an excellent likeness of the editor, who under the pen name of Alexander Blade had the lead novelet, "Carbon-Copy Killer," illustrated by Finlay.

Perhaps the most significant legacy of the Palmer years is Shaverism. In March 1945, Palmer began to publish a series by one Richard S. Shaver; the first story in the Shaver mystery series was called "'I Remember Lemuria'"—it was followed by 17 more through August 1947 (and more were published elsewhere thereafter).

Shaver was a problem. Many a writer had offered stories in which the narrators, as an auctorial device, would insist that their tales were based on actual events—readers would simply suspend their disbelief and go along for the ride. But Shaver (the author, not his narrators) claimed his stories were *true*. These stories featured evil underground degenerate cave-dwelling creatures called Deros that were supposed to be influencing humanity in a hateful fashion. Hordes of pseudo-fans were attracted to the Shaver stories like flies to a honeypot and, to the delight of the publishers and of editor Palmer, sales soared and Shaverism became a moneypot. Deros were the UFOs of their day: unsavory fiendish ogres. Meanwhile, out in the broader field of fandom, arguments were raging over the validity of Shaver's claims. Palmer backed him up, and of course the publisher was

(Opposite) July 1940

more interested in climbing sales figures than the dissatisfaction of hardcore fans. War raged in the science fiction field. When Palmer's editorship ended, he continued to support Shaver's fiction, but in the late '70s, Palmer did reveal that Shaver had been a patient in a state mental hospital where he was treated for paranoid schizophrenia.

Science Wonder Stories

When editor Hugo Gernsback lost his ownership of *Amazing Stories*, he immediately bounced back with a 25-cent sci-fi magazine every bit as exciting as his former periodical. It was called *Science Wonder Stories*, and the earliest editions in 1929 featured striking Frank R. Paul covers, supplemented by his awesome black-and-white interior illustrations. Gernsback published authors that the science fiction community had come to know and cherish: Jack Williamson, Stanton A. Coblentz, David H. Keller, Miles J. Breuer, Clifford D. Simak, Lawrence Manning, Ed Earl Repp, Francis Flagg, Henrik Dahl Juve—the list goes on and on. And those faithful fans who had subscribed before the first issue of the magazine appeared were handsomely rewarded with a per-copy price of 12½ cents—half its original price—*forever!*

The premier issue also announced the arrival of a quarterly—a companion sci-fi magazine, the aerially oriented *Air Wonder Stories*, with the same illustrator, same reputed authors! Alas, *Air Wonder Stories* lasted but 11 issues, and then combined with *Science Wonder Stories* to become plain old *Wonder Stories*.

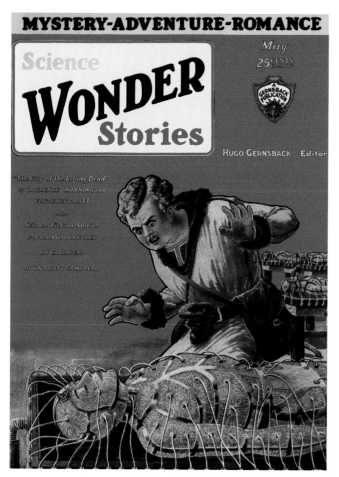

Top, Fall 1929; above, May 1930; opposite, May 1930

The INFINITE BRAIN
by John C. Campbell

JOHN C. CAMPBELL

I HAD known Anton Des Roubles, off and on, for more than fifteen years and was his closest and perhaps only friend. At least, no one else came to visit him, excepting collectors whom he paid regularly. He never went out to theaters or parties and apparently had no relatives.

I met him in 1923, when I was employed by a machinist's supply house with which he dealt, and so had occasion to take orders for and sometimes execute delicate work that he wanted. It was perhaps our mutual interest in mechanics that did the most towards bringing us together.

For my part I was immensely curious as to what Anton was working on. He seemed interested in automatons and derived considerable income from a patent covering an automatic time clock and burglar alarm system. His apartment was taken up mostly with a sort of laboratory, where he conducted various experiments. He was saved from expulsion from the apartment only by the high rent he paid. In fact his erratic turn of mind often led to annoying and sometimes grotesque results.

The people in the apartment below were constantly complaining about the hum of motors at all hours of the night, which complaints Anton silenced with pecuniary mufflers to the landlord. But one night matters came to a state where even money could not prevent trouble.

A number of young midnight revelers, returning from some roadhouse, came face to face with the most terrible apparition in the dim upper hall. It was shaped like a man but walked upon legs made of jointed steel rods. Its body, they said, looked like clockwork and it walked slowly and deliberately toward them. All were partly intoxicated and one of them grabbed the strange object. The thing at once struck him a terrific blow in the shoulder, throwing him to the floor. Later they told the police that it had stood still just like an animal at bay, and had waved its long feelers about, striking with lightning-like blows at whatever it touched. It hit another man, stunning him, and then struck the wall twice, after which it fell to the floor and lay still.

The young people, horrified at the thing, had fled downstairs, where the janitor notified the police. When the latter came in, the midnight wanderer was not in the hall; but it took little searching to locate it in Des Roubles' apart-

ment. Des Roubles was summoned to Court, but as no charge could be brought against him, he was released.

Reading the account of the episode in the papers, I went, on the morrow, to the apartment to see this mechanical wonder. With some pride my friend showed me the thing. It stood in a corner, suspended by a wire from the ceiling, like skeletons hung about in laboratories. One arm was off, lying on a bench where some repairs were being made. In place of a head, the weird thing had a score of rods, arranged in a circle, and connected to an equal number of long slender feelers of varying lengths. Anton, for once, was disposed to be communicative.

"You see," he explained, as we sat in his living room, enjoying our iced tea and cigars, "this machine is only the first step in what I am working toward. I suppose I am the only person in the world spending money upon such a fool thing, but I feel that every day brings me nearer my goal."

He smiled, and as he was evidently mellowed by my Corona cigar, I put a question I had long premeditated:

"But what are you working toward? I can't see any purpose, beyond novelty, in all this, Anton."

Anton laughed. "Really, Gene, I shouldn't keep you on pins and needles so long. I don't know why I haven't told you long ago. Well, now that the Press has part of my secret, there's no use hiding it any longer. I'll tell you all about it."

I leaned forward, wondering what he would say.

"You see, Gene," he began, "this is only a diversion, as it were, from my real work. The work itself is this: I am attempting to construct a mechanism exactly duplicating the mechanical and electrical processes occurring in the human brain and constituting the phenomena known as thought."

He stopped, observing my sudden surprise. "Now, that may sound rather deep, but it isn't really; at least the principle isn't. I am trying to make a mechanical brain, that will think, reason, remember, have likes and dislikes, loves and hates; that can read, write, appreciate a joke, or smoke a cigar."

I was perfectly amazed at the idea. In all that whirl of thoughts, I seized upon one I could understand. "But how could a cigar . . ."

Anton Explains

"TUSH! tush!" said Anton, "forget the cigar. I haven't attained my goal yet, so I don't know how a cigar would work. However, I have gone quite a way. I have

---

ONCE in a great while a story comes along that, for sheer originality and uniqueness, immediately commands respect.

We believe the present story to be one of this kind and in our opinion it is easily one of the great science fiction stories of the year.

The "Infinite Brain" is a tremendous story from beginning to end. Not only is it quite original but it is a dashing story of great adventure. And, if we do not miss our guess, it will be one of the most discussed stories of the year.

And lest you jump to the conclusion that intelligent, or quasi-intelligent, machines are pure figments of the imagination, remember that already, today, we have machines that can "think" faster and better than any human being. Adding, multiplying, and dividing machines and even machines to work problems in calculus do many things far better than the human brain can.

If you have visited a modern automatic telephone exchange, it will be brought home to you that, indeed, here is another intelligent machine that "thinks" straight and makes no mistakes.

There is in use today a tide-predicting and calculating machine used by the United States Government, which machine is universally recognized as doing the work of a number of men in calculating and solving the most intricate problems.

There is no question that, in the future, even more wonderful machines will be evolved along these lines.

It came suddenly, rushing with awful swiftness on the town. One great leg swung out with a push, breaking down telephone poles . . .

(Illustration by Paul)

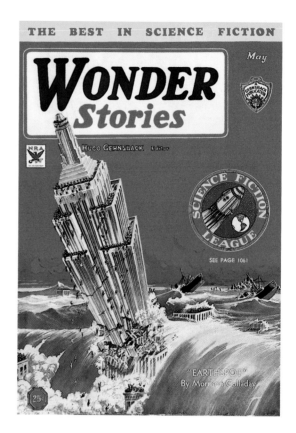

Left; November 1930; right,
May 1934

But—wonder of wonders!—in 1930, Gernsback introduced yet another science-oriented periodical, *Scientific Detective Monthly* (later renamed *Amazing Detective Tales*), which lasted only 10 issues. It featured contributions by Keller, Repp, and its editorial commissioner, Arthur B. Reeve. Reeve's stories were reprints that originally appeared in *Cosmopolitan* magazine between 1910 and 1918; the series was about Craig Kennedy, scientific detective, with stories like "The Body That Wouldn't Burn," "The Seismograph Adventure," "The Bacteriological Detective," and "The Terror in the Air."

February 1930

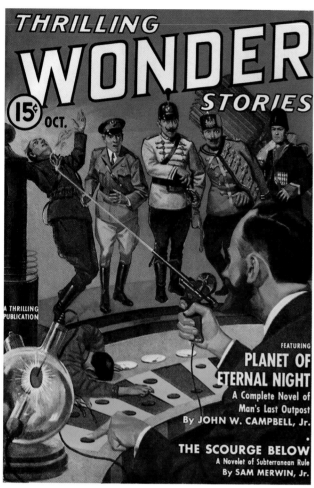

October 1939

Winter 1946

Thrilling Wonder Stories

Gernsback's *Wonder Stories* had bit the dust with its April 1936 issue but before long was back with a new editor (Mort Weisinger), format, fiction policy, and title. *Thrilling Wonder Stories* was basically a blood-and-thunder, thud-and-blunder periodical with no strong claim to scientific accuracy. Familiar names abounded: Arthur J. Burks, John Wood Campbell Jr., Ray Cummings, Ralph Milne Farley, Edmond Hamilton, Henry Kuttner, Murray Leinster, Frank Belknap Long, A. Merritt,

October 1936

August 1936

Stanley G. Weinbaum, Jack Williamson, Manley Wade Wellman, Arthur Leo Zagat.

Thrilling Wonder Stories kept fans apprised of the goings-on of the Science Fiction League. Other features included a free Swap column; the ScientiBook Review column; and, for awhile, a column called The Story Behind the Story, which featured revelations by the authors as to how their stories had come about. There was also a short-lived picture-story feature, which today I would term a scientificomic strip, entitled *Zarnak* by Max Plaisted. *Zarnak* was a poor man's *Flash Gordon*.

Thrilling Wonder Stories continued month after month, year after year, virtually unchanged, obviously

From the October 1939 issue of *Thrilling Wonder Stories*, the leading personalities of the First World Science Fiction Convention. Top row, left to right: Sam Moskowitz (director of the convention), Will S. Sykora, James V. Taurasi, Forrest J Ackerman (yours truly). Bottom row, left to right: Jack Darrow, Morojo (Myrtle Douglas), Julius Schwartz, Mario Racic Jr.

Spring 1944

giving its readership what it wanted. There were, of course, occasional letters of comment by Forrest J Ackerman.

The October 1939 number reviewed the First World Science Fiction Convention in glowing terms and had one page with photos of eight of the participants. At least five of them—Sam Moskowitz, Will S. Sykora, James V. Taurasi, Morojo, and Mario Racic Jr., a "scientifilm expert"—are now dead. No one seems to know what became of Jack Darrow. The other two, Julius Schwartz and myself, still appear to be alive.

Thrilling Wonder Stories chugged along until 1955, as did its companion publication, *Startling Stories* (founded in January 1939), which was virtually the same magazine under a different title.

January 1930

Editorial from January 1930

Astounding
THE BATES ERA

The year 1930 started off right with the introduction of a new science fiction magazine to rival *Amazing Stories* and *Science Wonder Stories*. *Astounding Stories of Super-Science* never developed a quarterly as did its rival publications, but this new 20-cent pulp immediately became a strong contender in the sci-fi field. Its editor, Harry Bates, would become famous for his story "Farewell to

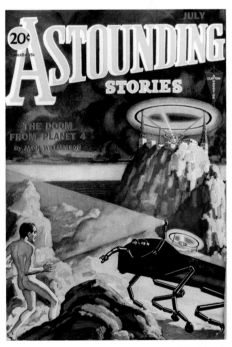

July 1931

the Master," which became the classic scientifilm *The Day the Earth Stood Still.* Popular artist Wesso drew the first cover and stories were featured by such well-known names of the day as Ray Cummings, Murray Leinster, and Victor Rousseau.

Astounding's first year had many highlights.

In the February 1930 issue, *Astounding* published its first female writer, Sophie Wenzel Ellis (who 20 years later became one of my clients).

In the August 1930 issue, author Jack Williamson, in the letters section, writes of a previous issue that he enjoyed the whole magazine and found "the literary quality surprisingly high." (Toward the end of the 20th century, Jack Williamson's high-quality stories continue to be published.)

In the November 1930 issue, P. Schuyler Miller has a long scholarly letter, characterizing himself as a science fiction fan, a student of chemistry, and a hopeful author. (In April 1936, he finally cracked the pages of *Astounding* with "The Chrysalis" and for years was the most popular book reviewer the magazine ever published.)

November 1937

One year after its inception, *Astounding Stories of Super-Science* became simply *Astounding Stories.* Toward the end of the year, there appeared a long novelette named "Hawk Carse," a space opera story that took the readers by storm. Three more Carse tales followed and engendered a guessing game of galactic proportions: Who was the mysterious author Anthony Gilmore? As late as 1934, fans were speculating on Gilmore's identity. When I asked for his autograph on a card—as I did in those days of most every sci-fi writer—I received a typewritten note: "But Anthony Gilmore is *two* men!" Eventually the collaborators were revealed to be none other than editor Harry Bates and his assistant, Desmond W. Hall. In 1932 all four stories were preserved in hardcover as *Space Hawk*.

By mid-1932, economic hardships required that *Astounding* scale down, so it went bimonthly; and with the March 1933 issue it folded, temporarily.

THE TREMAINE ERA

At the end of 1933 *Astounding* was back with a 34-year-old editor at its helm (F. Orlin Tremaine) and new publishers (Street & Smith). The November issue startled readers with a full-page announcement that the next issue would contain "a story that will awaken more controversy than any story ever published in a science-fiction magazine." It was "Ancestral Voices" by Nat Schachner and became the first of a series of "thought variant" stories of which the editor wrote, "Our purpose is to bring to you each month one story carrying a new and unexplored 'thought variant' in the field of scientific fiction." The late Alva Rogers in his watershed work, *A Requiem for Astounding,* calls the first thought-variant "a remarkable story and one of the first of the sociologically oriented type of science fiction that dominated the '40s."

Another thought-variant story was Donald Wandrei's "Colossus" (January 1934), of a protagonist who expanded his body until it became so gigantic that he burst through the limits of our universe and found himself in a greater universe in which ours was but an atom. The March 1934 issue featured *two* thought variants, "The Man Who Stopped the Dust" (with disastrous

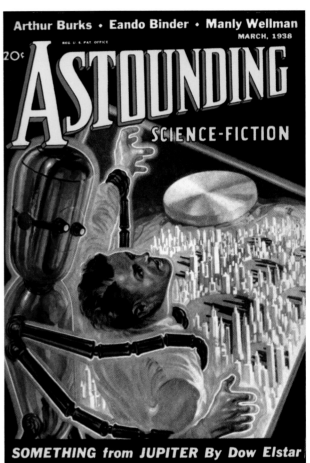

March 1938

results) by British author John Russell Fearn and "Born of the Sun" by none other than Jack Williamson (the issue was also notable because its page count increased from 144 to 160 while retaining its popular 20-cent price, a nickel less than its competitors). Other thought-variant stories were Nat Schachner's "He from Procyon" (April 1934) and Murray Leinster's "Sidewise in Time" (June 1934).

Between 1935 and 1937 *Astounding* published such memorable works as John Taine's novel-length serial "Twelve Eighty-Seven"; numerous shorts by John Campbell writing as Don A. Stuart; a number of Weinbaum classics; *Weird Tales* favorite H. P. Lovecraft with his famous "At the Mountains of Madness" and "The Shadow Out of Time"; and Harry Bates's tour de force of three million years hence and the end of genus *Homo superior*, "Alas, All Thinking." In 1937, L. Sprague de Camp and Eric Frank Russell made their auctorial bows and would be favorites for decades to come. Self-exiled German rocket pioneer Willy Ley contributed exemplary science articles.

THE CAMPBELL ERA

Beginning in November 1937, author and brand-new editor John Wood Campbell Jr. gave us a Golden Age, a pyrotechnical cornucopia of the top sci-fi authors of all time and their glorious stories. Campbell introduced the following classic titles to a receptive, ever-growing audience: Isaac Asimov's "Nightfall" and *Foundation* series; Robert Heinlein's "By His Bootstraps" (under the pseudonym Anson MacDonald); "Fifty Million Monkeys" and "Renaissance" by Raymond F. Jones; Henry Kuttner's "Mimsy Were the Borogoves" (under the pseudonym Lewis Padgett); C. L. Moore's "No Woman Born"; Theodore Sturgeon's "Killdozer"; and A. E. van Vogt's "Slan" and "Black Destroyer."

In addition, Campbell published high-quality fiction

by established writers: His own "Who Goes There?" (the basis for *The Thing*) under the pen name Don A. Stuart; "Metamorphosite" by Eric Frank Russell; and E. E. Smith's "Children of the Lens" are some of my favorites. Ray Bradbury also contributed three stories to *Astounding* during Campbell's reign: "Eat, Drink, and Be Wary" (July 1942), "And Watch the Fountains Play" (September 1942), and "Doodad" (September 1943).

The magazine became *Astounding Science Fiction* in March 1938, and then *Analog Science Fiction–Science Fact* in 1960. Today, it is simply referred to as *Analog*. Over the years, it has published hundreds of excellent authors; those I mentioned are merely the cream of the crop. But one other name comes to mind from the Campbell era: L. Ron Hubbard.

Hubbard's very first story, "The Dangerous Dimension," was published in the July 1938 edition of *Astounding*. His most popular *Astounding* stories were "Final Blackout" (April 1940)—a story of loyalty to the Lieutenant during World War 33, which Robert Heinlein hailed as "the perfect science fiction story"—and the Doc Methuselah series (1947–1950). When Hubbard wrote the nonfiction *Dianetics: The Modern Science of Mental Health* in 1950 (the forerunner of today's Church of Scientology), A. E. van Vogt, for one, embraced Dianetics with great enthusiasm. *Dianetics*, the book, has become a perennial, having sold millions of copies in the last five decades, and *it*, rather than his sci-fi stories, is definitely what Hubbard will be remembered for.

Campbell remained a strong supporter of Hubbard despite great cynicism and flak on the part of readers and critics. But *Astounding* did not really suffer in

July 1964

L. RON HUBBARD

My wife, Wendayne, and I were well acquainted with L. Ron Hubbard.

I was Hubbard's literary agent for a short time before the advent of Dianetics: "To the Stars" (in *Astounding Science Fiction*, February 1950) and "Masters of Sleep" (*Fantastic Adventures*, October 1950) were two of the better works I helped him publish. But I never considered the majority of his stories more than adequate diversions. Hubbard never wrote a classic science fiction masterpiece of erudite philosophy and social responsibility, a blueprint for a better tomorrow. He simply wrote some entertaining stories. Ron personally was very good to me; he amazingly volunteered that I should take 50% commission on his reprint sales during the last decade of his life.

His current literary representatives, with unlimited funds, have performed miracles. He has by now been translated around the world into as many languages as Edgar Rice Burroughs, including Chinese, and he's got his own museum on Hollywood Boulevard.

I'm no supporter of Dianetics and Scientology, but I did have some firsthand experiences early on in the movement that have left a favorable impression on me, despite other things that bring out the cynic in me.

For instance, after I suffered a series of heart attacks on the way to my 50th birthday celebration, A. E. van Vogt kindly volunteered to give me free recuperative Dianetic sessions, and I believe they did me some good.

Wendayne graduated from Hubbard's initial Dianetics course in Los Angeles and became one of the first authenticated auditors. She cured my canine phobia in quick order; eventually I even petted a full-grown lion.

Also during this time, I watched Wendayne help a woman who, over several years, had spent thousands of dollars on psychiatrists for her grown daughter without tangible results; my wife got to the core of the daughter's psychosis in a couple of interesting—and inexpensive—sessions, and released her from her erratic behavior syndrome. Wendayne was dedicated and actually accomplished minor miracles with individuals not only in Los Angeles but in London. She eventually gave it up because being a dedicated auditor was too draining on her.

the long run because Campbell was committed to maintaining the high quality of the fiction, and he did so until his death in 1971. Upon Campbell's death, Jack Williamson said, "Science fiction was his life.... Wells established and defined the genre.... Gernsback named it; Campbell is the third major name in its history. In the whole domain of science fiction, we are all his debtors."

The Other Pulps

Super Science Stories arrived in March 1940, favoring many of editor Frederik Pohl's friends as contributors. The name changed to *Super Science Novels* for three issues in 1941, but reverted to its original moniker until it folded in 1943. It was given a second life, coming out 15 times between January 1949 and August 1951 under the editorship of Ejler Jakobsson. Both Pohl and Jakobsson would later serve as editors of *Galaxy* (see page 133).

Comet Stories, under former *Astounding* editor F. Orlin Tremaine, issued five numbers between December 1940 and July 1941, and disgraced itself by failing to provide the prize as offered for the fan traveling the greatest distance to the World Science Fiction Convention of 1941.

Famous Fantastic Mysteries was published for around 15 years, starting in late 1939, under the editorship of

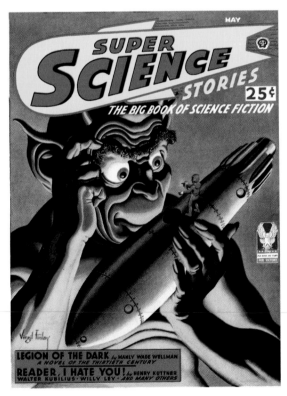

May 1943

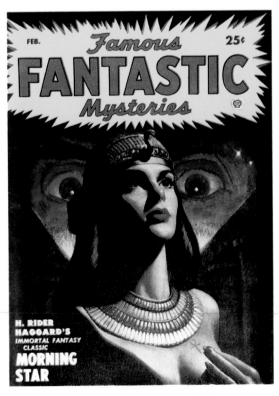

February 1950

May 1943

April–May 1939

Spring 1940

Mary Gnaedinger. The publisher, Frank A. Munsey, was responsible for *Argosy* and *All-Story* between the late 1800s and the 1920s; *FFM* reprinted famous "Argosyarns" by the likes of Ray Cummings, George Allen England, Homer Eon Flint, Austin Hall, A. Merritt, and Francis Stevens, with handsome illustrations by the Master, Frank R. Paul, as well as Virgil Finlay and Lawrence. Its companion, *Fantastic Novels*, featured longer works by the early masters.

Science Fiction appeared in March 1939 and *Future Fiction* the following November under the aegis of the boy wonder Charles D. Hornig (who in '33 had become editor of *Wonder Stories* at the age of 17). The former folded after 12 issues, and the latter after 17. Hornig's successor, Robert A. W. Lowndes, gave *Future Science Fiction* a second life between 1950 and 1960. Few stories were memorable but artwork by Frank R. Paul and Hannes Bok was welcome.

Marvel (Marvel Science Stories, Marvel Tales, and *Marvel Stories* between 1938 and 1941; then *Marvel Stories* and *Marvel Science Fiction* in its 1950–1952 incarnation) is famous for "Survival" by Arthur J. Burks and its sequel, "Exodus," two powerful future war stories, and its one-issue attempt to combine science and sex with racy tales by Burks, Ray Cummings and Jack Williamson, Cummings (as Ray King), and Williamson (as himself and as Nils O. Sonderlund).

Planet Stories, first published in late 1939, featured "interplanetaryarns," including some good ones by Isaac Asimov, Leigh Brackett, Ray Bradbury, and Albert DePiña. Sometime in the '40s, its socially conscious, ahead-of-his-time editor, Paul Payne, published a story by an equally liberal author who introduced a black character who was *not* in some subservient role (or used only for comic relief as in the motion pictures of the time). This black man was a fully fleshed human being on a par with the other planeteers of the plot. An irate bigot wrote to the readers' department, The Vizigraph, and blew his top over the elevation of a black man to human status. Numerous readers took offense, including one whose name identified him as a likely Jew. The bigot lashed back in a subsequent Vizigraph, ranting that Jews were in the same subhuman category as Negroes. The Jew actually bought a roundtrip ticket, flew from Los Angeles to the city of the offending individual, took a taxi to his residence, knocked on his apartment door, socked him on the jaw, returned to the waiting taxi, and took the next flight back home.

Boucher and Gold

In the 1950s, two distinctly different personalities entered the scene as editors, approximately a year apart. Both had previously been known only as authors, and excellent ones at that; now they were at the helm of what were to be two of the most important sci-fi magazines of all time: Anthony Boucher's *Magazine of Fantasy and Science Fiction* and H. L. Gold's *Galaxy*. Boucher was as sweet and gentle and considerate an editor as ever has graced the genre; Gold was as irascible and ego-bruising as the Marquis incarnate. "Ackerman, you are a basket case of acrimony!" he once accused me, erroneously believing me responsible for a harsh criticism of *Galaxy*. (At a later date he got up from a luncheon table, asked me if I would be his agent, and kissed me on the forehead.) It might be said that as Fritz Lang was to films, Gold was to magazines; as Peter Cushing was in real life, Boucher was in editorial. Both produced superior publications. Gold tended toward the sociological and psychological, offering dazzling masterpieces by Ray Bradbury ("The Fireman, " on which *Fahrenheit 451* was based), Robert Heinlein ("Year of the Jackpot"), Richard Matheson ("Shipshape Home"), Theodore Sturgeon ("Baby Is Three"), Alfred Bester ("The Stars My Destination"), Pohl and Kornbluth ("The Space

November 1950

January 1976

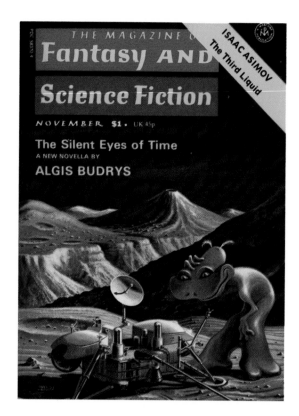

January 1951, November 1975

Merchants"), and many more while Boucher was matching with classics by John Anthony ("The Hypnoglyph"), G. Gordon Dewey ("The Tooth"—a unique tale told from the ending backward), Philip K. Dick ("The Father-Thing"), Philip Jose Farmer ("The Alley Man"), Damon Knight ("A for Anything"), Fritz Leiber ("The Silver Eggheads"), and scores more.

In the '50s, *Galaxy* did what other upstarts had not been able to do throughout the '30s and '40s—it gave *Astounding Science Fiction* a run for its money. It lasted until 1980. *The Magazine of Fantasy and Science Fiction* is still going strong; it has made a strong case for the literary validity of science fiction as a genre. In the words of John Clute in his *Science Fiction: The Illustrated Encyclopedia,* "*FSF* would be recognized as the home, for half a century, of many of America's best short stories."

In recent years, Kristine Kathryn Rusch did an exemplary job as editor of *Fantasy and Science Fiction* until she resigned to devote her talents to writing. She was one of the BOAT (best-of-all-time) female editors, sailing alongside Cele Goldsmith (*Amazing*), Mary Gnaedinger (*Famous Fantastic Mysteries*), and Bea Mahaffey (*Other Worlds* and *Imagination*).

The British Are Coming

In the 1950s, England got into the act with three British sci-fi publications, *Tales of Wonder*, *New Worlds*, and *Authentic Science Fiction*, which both reprinted American fiction and presented such homegrown talents as Arthur C. Clarke, Eric Frank Russell, and William F. Temple. *Nebula Science Fiction* was issued from Scotland and had a mixture similar to that of *Authentic*. I had a regular Scientifilm column in *Nebula* and an American Commentary column in *Authentic*.

February 1953

SF FILM NEWS DIRECT FROM HOLLYWOOD

April 1955

Sci-Fi on the
Silver Screen

Spaceward Bound

One of the earliest scientifilms is an 1899 three-minute short, *A Trip to the Moon (La Lune à un Mètre)* by the pioneering special-effects wizard, director Georges Méliès. Three years later, Méliès made a 21-minute *Trip to the Moon (Le Voyage dans la Lune)*, but this one was based on works by Jules Verne (*From the Earth to the Moon*, 1865) and H. G. Wells (*The First Men in the Moon*, 1901). Méliès's *Trip* survives to this day and is one of the most frequently seen films of nearly 100 years ago. The Selenites, hopping about like grasshoppers on a hot tin roof, are a scream, and the Man in the Moon getting poked in the eye by the rocket is a comedic classic.

The British cinemadapted H. G. Wells's *First Men in the Moon* in 1919, and the next year the popular Bray Studios gave America a silent short entitled *First Man to the Moon*. Even earlier (1917), a Danish *Sky Ship* featured a rocket flight to Mars, the discovery on the Red Planet of a Utopian society, and the transportation back to Earth of a Martian emissary. (I have actually seen this rare title, projected for me by the film library of the Cinémathèque in Brussels.) The Bray Studios were back in 1922 with a highly imaginative interplanetary one-reeler, *The Sky Splitter*, about

In 1968, the public was bombarded with the image advertising *2001: A Space Odyssey*; MGM plastered it everywhere in an attempt to recoup its $10.5 million investment in the film (opposite). Below, the central image from Méliès's *A Trip to the Moon (Le Voyage dans la lune)*.

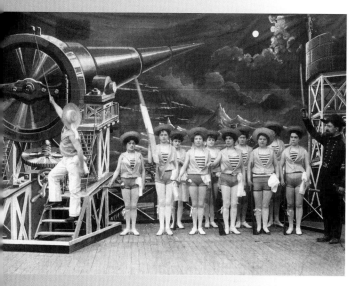

Images from a trio of early scientifilms. From top to bottom: A group of astronautic chorus girls in *A Trip to the Moon*; the star of *The Sky Splitter* (1922); and director Fritz Lang (directly behind camera) shooting a scene for *Die Frau im Mond* (*The Girl in the Moon*).

a faster-than-light rocket. When it landed on a far distant planet, the pilot looked through a telescope—and observed himself coming!

Pre-1930 interplanetary/interstellar voyages included *A Trip to Mars* (four times beginning in 1903, with a Thomas Edison version in 1910 complete with Martians and tree-monsters, and simultaneous Danish and Italian trips in 1920). *Around a Star* (French, 1906) transported an astronomer in a soap bubble; and the Soviets got in the act (naturally going to the Red Planet) in 1924 with *Aelita: The Revolt of the Robots*, a comedy about a Martian queen, loosely based on a Tolstoy story. The film still exists—it may be found in major video shops—and is memorable mainly for the sartorial styles of the Martians. That same year Bray made us get *All Aboard for the Moon* via a chemically propelled rocket.

In 1923, audiences thrilled to *M.A.R.S.* (also known as *Mars Calling*, *The Man from Mars*, and *Radio-Mania*), the first sci-fi film photographed in 3-D. In a dream sequence, an inventor finds himself in communication with Martians. They impart various secrets to him from their advanced civilization, such as a process by which coal can be transmuted into diamonds as big as eggs, and gold created from common clay. The Martians were pictured as large-headed individuals with huge ears, with mentalities a millennium in advance of terrestrials.

In his 1929 film *Die Frau im Mond* (released in the U.K. as *The Girl in the Moon* and in the U.S. as *By Rocket to the Moon*), Austrian director Fritz "Metropolis" Lang invented the countdown: 10—9—8—7—6—5—4—3—2—1—liftoff!

The '30s and '40s gave us relatively few interplanetary voyages: *Flash Gordon* (1936), who's from the planet Mongo; the sequel *Flash Gordon's Trip to Mars* (1938); and *Buck Rogers* (1939), in which Buck visits Saturn in the 25th century, were the biggest successes. The '40s offered *Flash Gordon Conquers the Universe* (1940), alien possession in *The Purple Monster Strikes* (1945), and *Superman* from Krypton (1948). (If you're wondering why—amid

this proliferation of silver screen renderings of comic book superheroes—some movies have been omitted, remember that *The Adventures of Captain Marvel* (1941), *Batman* (1943), and *Captain America* (1944) did not involve space travel, and that the fiction was more fantasy than science.)

Space travel really took off in the 1950s. Nineteen

Buster Crabbe as Flash Gordon (top) and as Buck Rogers (bottom). To the left is a scene from *Destination Moon*, George Pal's vision of the first landing on the moon as coscripted by Robert A. Heinlein from his own novel *Rocketship Galileo*.

years before *Apollo 11* and the first real moonwalk, *Destination Moon* gave us a remarkably realistic account of the first landing and won a special-effects Oscar in 1950; Robert Heinlein was one of the writers. Another 1950 production, director Kurt Neumann's *Rocketship X-M*, is about a flight to the moon that accidentally ends up on Mars.

Three classics came in 1951, to the delight of sci-fi buffs everywhere! In Robert Wise's *The Day the Earth Stood Still*, non-Earthlings arrive in Washington, D.C., to warn us about our self-destruction via the A-bomb. In producer Howard Hawks's *The Thing* (based on a John W. Campbell story), scientists and servicemen at an Air Force base in Antarctica thaw a buried saucer, only to be stalked by its nonhuman, plantlike carnivore inhabitant. And in *When Worlds Collide*, based on Philip Wylie's novel, Earth is actually destroyed (although a handful of survivors journey to the planet Zyra, which ain't so bad after all).

(Top) Rockets really got rolling in the '50s, starting with *Rocketship X-M* (1950), which took viewers on a wild ride as its spaceship veered off course and landed on Mars. In 1951, 20th Century-Fox delivered the first of its classic sci-fi films: *The Day the Earth Stood Still* was a surprisingly convincing plea for nuclear disarmament, and made a worldwide star out of both Michael Rennie and Gort, the huge robot under his control (opposite page). Director Robert Wise (shown above) revisited the nuclear device theme (and mixed it with a deadly virus) in 1971's *The Andromeda Strain*.

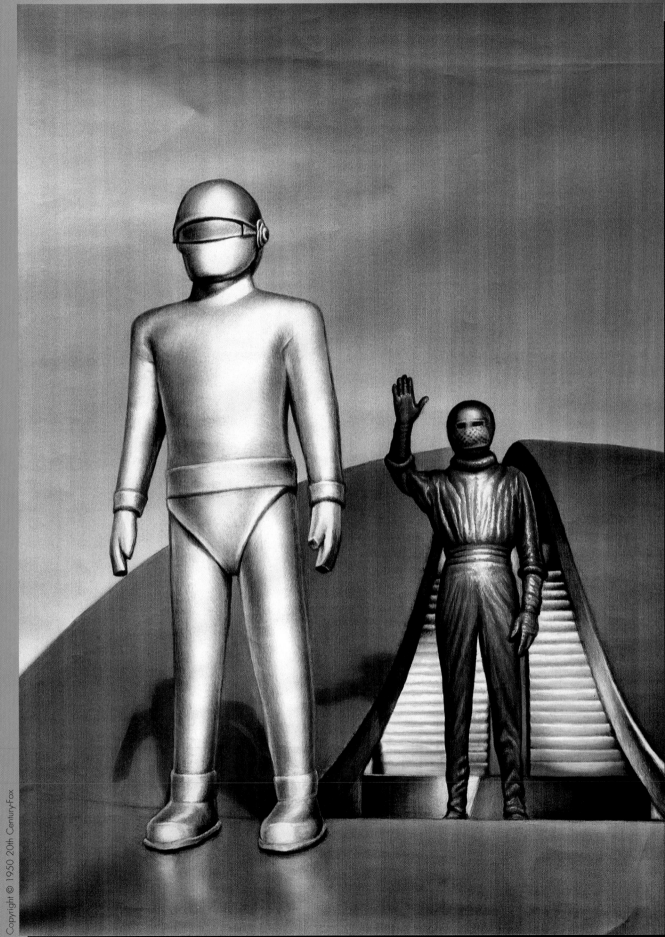

George Pal, who produced *Destination Moon* and *When Worlds Collide*, delivered the screen version of H. G. Wells's *War of the Worlds* in 1954, in which a mass invasion of Martians cannot be stopped by human manpower. Unfortunately for the Martians, they have no immunities to earthly bacteria and die.

Britain's Hammer Films had great success in 1955 with *The Quatermass Xperiment*, in which an astronaut crashes and, during his supposed convalescence, becomes a living fungus. The 1957 *Quatermass II* adds government conspiracy to the alien invasion/biological catastrophe mix, and is considered a classic.

George Pal (1908–1980) was one of the great figures of the science fiction film genre. Born in Hungary and trained in architecture, he moved to Berlin to design sets for UFA. Did he work on the sets for *Metropolis*? Perhaps. He moved to Hollywood in 1940, introduced the Puppetoon series, and went on to produce five films that won special-effects Oscars: *Destination Moon* (1950), *When Worlds Collide* (1951), *War of the Worlds* (1953), *Tom Thumb* (1958), and *The Time Machine* (1960).

Copyright © 1958 Allied Artists Pictures

WOMEN IN SCIENTIFILMS

For better or for worse, the role of women in sci-fi films started to change in the late '50s. Generally speaking, early sci-fi films had neither heroines nor female menaces—women had been victims waiting to be protected from the bad guys (or aliens) by the good guys. All that began to change in camp classics such as

Fire Maidens from Outer Space (1956), in which descendants of Atlantis are all near Jupiter and are all female (near right, center), except for a single aged man.

Queen of Outer Space (1958), in which a Venusian queen (Zsa Zsa Gabor, left) kills all the men on her planet before attempting to destroy the planet Earth.

I Married a Monster from Outer Space (1958), in which aliens who need to procreate for the sake of their dying home planet come to Earth, assume human form, and pose as lookalike bridegrooms—until one new bride catches on (near right, top).

Attack of the 50 Foot Woman (1958), in which a genetically altered woman goes giant (right) and ends up with her husband (and his mistress) in the palm of her hand.

ATTACK OF THE 50 FT. WOMAN

starring ALLISON HAYES · WILLIAM HUDSON · YVETTE VICKERS · PRODUCED BY BERNARD WOOLNER
DIRECTED BY NATHAN HERTZ · WRITTEN BY MARK HANNA · AN ALLIED ARTISTS PICTURE

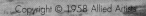

Not since William Cameron Menzies directed *Things to Come* had such a tweeky individual made a science fiction film. With elegant compositions, music, sets, and incidents (such as Astronaut Poole receiving prerecorded birthday greetings from his parents via videophone, right), Kubrick dared to suggest that space travel would be dull—and dangerous.

It was Stanley Kubrick's *2001: A Space Odyssey* (1968) that forever changed the space film. The screenplay was cowritten by Kubrick and the great science fiction writer Arthur C. Clarke. Unlike previous space films that were made during the Cold War to convince us of our superiority (didn't the aliens always suffer, even if they

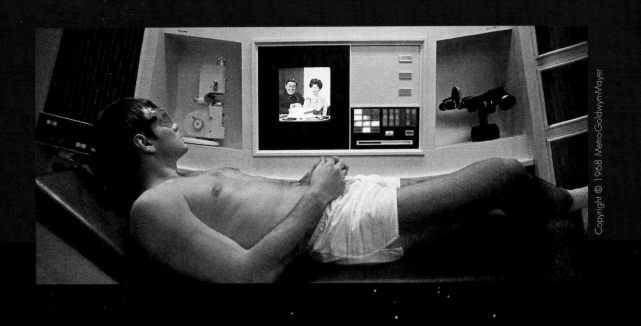

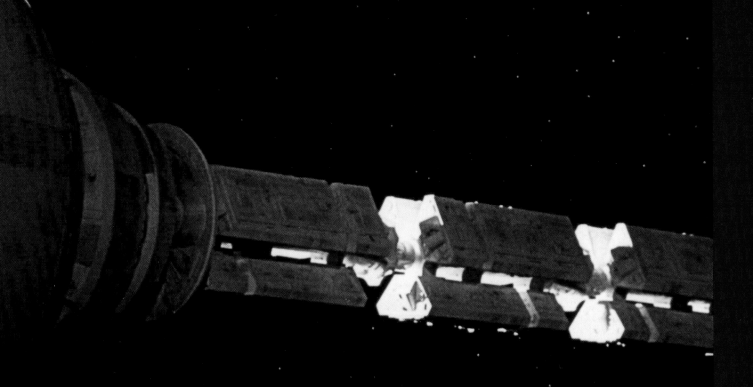

terrorized us temporarily?), this was a movie more concerned with mankind's humble place in this vast universe and our ongoing spiritual quest. How terrifying that the antagonist was *not* some evil lunar monster but rather was an artificial intelligence computer created by man himself! The film *2001* explores (among many other things) what we have done to ourselves, and where we are going—physically and philosophically.

The United States and the Soviet Union had been

sending manned vehicles into orbit since 1961, but when this film was made no one had yet landed on the moon (the historic *Apollo* mission in which Armstrong took the first moonwalk did not occur until July 1969). And so popular interest in astronauts and technology was just about to reach an all-time high. With *2001* the question was no longer, What if there is someone out there?—filmmakers had been asking that for years. Kubrick and Clarke presented two far more interesting questions that tapped into the space-hungry public at large: What if there isn't? Or what if there is and it's not what we had imagined?

This film is not universally loved. No one would deny that it influenced the look and scale of every space story to follow—from *Star Wars* to *Contact*. But many find it pretentious and cryptic—this is not straight story-telling by any means, and its ambiguities and open-endedness are not everyone's cup of tea. The final third of the movie is a psyche-delic tour de force (this *was* the '60s): Light and speed and time had never been visually represented this way before, and for audience members as well as astronauts Poole (Gary Lockwood) and Bowman (Keir Dullea), this was a "trip." But those who appreciate this film consider it not just one of the best pictures of the '60s or a great sci-fi epic—they consider it one of the best films of all time.

In the wake of *Dr. Strangelove* (1964), 39-year-old Bronx-born Stanley Kubrick (far left, top) had acquired a "certain reputation," and MGM wrote him and Arthur C. Clarke a very big ticket to produce *2001: A Space Odyssey*. Meticulously researched throughout the technological world, the film realistically presented the world of commercial space travel, from the mundanities of waiting-lounge pleasantries (below left, in a bizarrely colored lobby card from the original release) to the amount one would pay for a phone call back home. The vast and stately beauty of the special effects won the film many admirers, as well as an Oscar for Kubrick. His use of classical music was the result of "temp love": He had edited the picture to the music you hear in the film, but it had an original score written for it that was later discarded. For years, the film's original Cinerama, Super Panavision, and Metrocolor presentation has been severely crippled on TV. It wasn't until recently that the Voyager Company put out a letterbox laserdisc of the film, which promptly became a best-seller.

In 1976, director Nicolas Roeg delivered *The Man Who Fell to Earth*. It starred David Bowie, Rip Torn, Buck Henry, and Candy Clark (an Oscar nominee for her performance in George Lucas's 1973 smash, *American Graffiti*) in a fascinating over-the-top performance as a floozy who falls for Bowie's Thomas Jerome Newton (who she at first thinks is fully human). Newton has left his wife and children on their drought-ridden planet in search of water. His planet appears doomed despite its technological superiority, so with a handful of revolutionary patents, he sets up a trillion-dollar industrial empire in the United States, with the long-term goal of rescuing his home planet via an interplanetary water-

shipping industry. Earthly fear and cynicism
abound when Newton's mysterious origins are
investigated, and in our terrestrial attempts to humanize
Newton, we turn him into a caged, bored, alcohol-depen-
dent, video-obsessed business magnate who never gets
home. The story is based on the 1963 novel by Walter
Tevis, and is one of the finer treatments in which the aliens
are not simply grotesques with purely evil intentions, and
our own earthly capacity for malice is addressed.

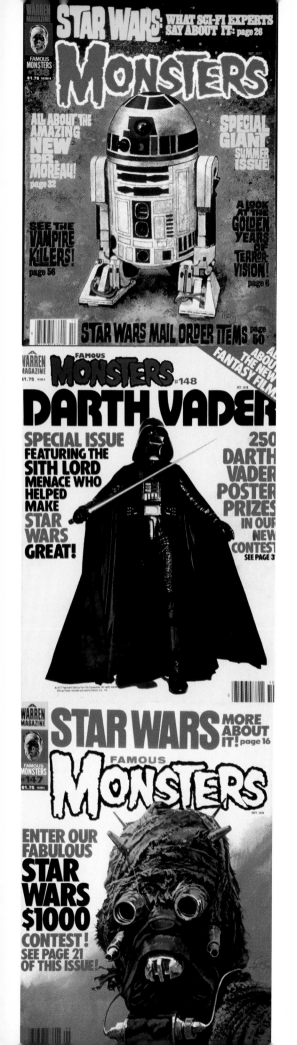

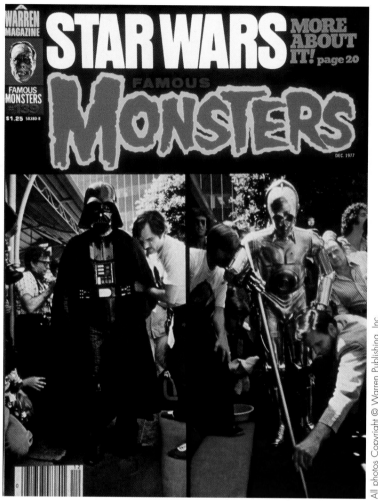

In 1977, something truly amazing happened in the world of science fiction and the world of motion pictures. That something was the one-two punch of George Lucas's *Star Wars* and Steven Spielberg's *Close Encounters of the Third Kind*. Both films built upon the revolutionary visuals of Kubrick's *2001* but lacked that film's deliberate artiness: These were storytelling for the whole family. And science fiction films became Hollywood's biggest blockbusters.

Lucas followed *Star Wars* with two sequels—1980's *The Empire Strikes Back* and 1983's *Return of the Jedi*. In 1997, the trilogy was rereleased as the *Star Wars Special Edition*, restored with a state-of-the-art digital

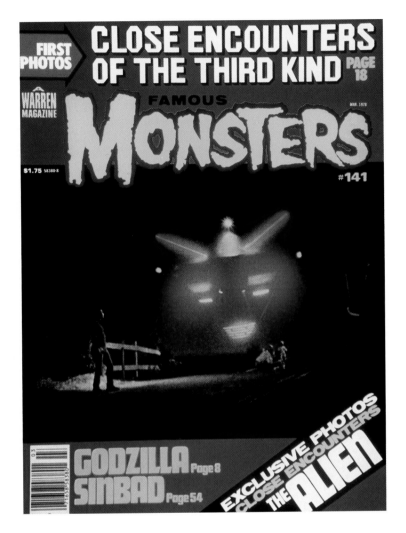

The unprecedented popularity of both George Lucas's *Star Wars* and Steven Spielberg's *Close Encounters of the Third Kind* generated both a new interest in sci-fi and a new respectability among studio executives. The public was equally fascinated with the processes by which these films were created and the behind-the-scenes personalities responsible for them. Most people know, for instance, that John Williams wrote the music for both films. (In the case of *Star Wars*, he did so for a percentage of the profits.) As *Star Wars* played for over a year at the Chinese Theater in Hollywood, packed houses of the faithful would gather on weekends yelling *"Turn it up!"* David Prowse, as Darth Vader, and Anthony Daniels, as C-3PO (both pictured on the *Famous Monsters* cover on the opposite page), got to put their footprints in the theater's famed forecourt.

soundtrack, enhanced special effects, and new footage. After its January 1997 rerelease, *Star Wars* topped Spielberg's *E.T. The Extra-Terrestrial* (1982) as the all-time domestic box office champ at $460 million (*E.T.*'s is at $407 million). The new and improved *Empire* came out the following February and *Jedi* that March; both are firmly fixed in the top 10, with *Empire* at number 8 (having grossed $290 million) and *Jedi* at number 6 (with $307 million).

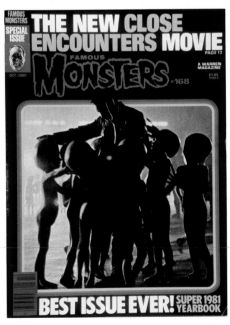

Icons from "a long time ago in a galaxy far, far away" (clockwise from above) Luke Skywalker, Princess Leia, and Han Solo; Darth Vader; R2-D2 and C-3PO; and the Grand Moff Tarkin.

Star Wars set the standard for science fiction fantasy design and special-effects work. The incredible battle sequences between Imperial Tie fighters (right) and the rebel X-wing fighters (center) were inspired by filmed newsreels of WW II air battles and edited together by Paul Hirsch, Marcia Lucas, and Richard Chew. The effects work was all supervised by John Dykstra at the newly created Industrial Light and Magic. A tilt-slab warehouse in the San Fernando Valley, ILM marked the beginning of a new chapter in the history of motion pictures.

After *Star Wars* broke box office records, Lucas and Industrial Light and Magic pulled up stakes and moved to Marin County. Lucas swore he would never direct again, and sat down with Lawrence Kasdan to write and produce the $30 million sequel *The Empire Strikes Back*. This film introduced even more unforgettable characters such as Yoda (above), an incredibly old Jedi master who teaches Luke about the Force, and Lando Calrussian, who offers Chewbacca and Han Solo much-needed refuge (left, bottom). When *The Return of the Jedi* came out, we finally got to see what Jabba the Hut looked like (left, top). Below, one of the many ILM model makers readies a ship for its close-up.

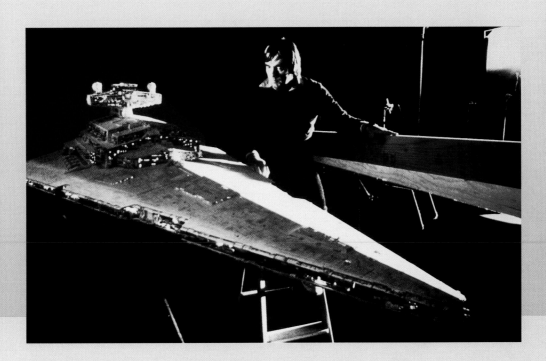

STEVEN SPIELBERG

Steven Spielberg has had an amazing career, in and out of sci-fi. Although he is mainly known as a film director, he got his first big break in TV on *Rod Serling's Night Gallery*; has written or cowritten a number of his TV and film projects; and as a film producer, has delivered a number of successful fantasy adventures that others directed—for example, Tobe Hooper's *Poltergeist* (1982), Joe Dante's *Gremlins* (1984), and Richard Donner's *The Goonies* (1985). Spielberg is perhaps Hollywood's most successful jack-of-all-trades, master-of-all.

But it is his success as a director that is amazing and astounding. These are but some of the highlights:

His suspense thriller *Jaws* (1975) rests at number 10 of the top 50 all-time highest grossing movies, with a total intake of $260 million. This is truly awesome when one considers that tickets then cost half of what they do today. Three *Jaws* sequels followed, but none had the Spielberg touch.

Close Encounters of the Third Kind (1977), Spielberg's first alien-contact film, won two Academy Awards: for cinematography (Vilmos Zsigmond) and sound-effects editing (Frank Warner). It was also nominated for best director (Spielberg), best supporting actress (Melinda Dillon), and a host of technical awards. John Williams's original score lost to…John Williams's score for *Star Wars*.

Copyright © 1983 Amblin Entertainment, Inc.

Spielberg's action-adventure trilogy—*Raiders of the Lost Ark* (1981), *Indiana Jones and the Temple of Doom* (1984), and *Indiana Jones and the Last Crusade* (1989)—has cumulatively grossed more than $620 million at the box office.

His sci-fi blockbuster *E.T. The Extra-Terrestrial* (1982) is the work with which he's most associated and for which he's most appreciated. He brought to life a character from outer space that appealed to kids and adults, males and females—and told a story that appealed to more than just the typical sci-fi fan. Young Drew Barrymore made a particularly impressive movie debut. With box office receipts of more than $400 million, it is fixed at number 2 behind *Star Wars*. (Number 3 on the list is Spielberg's *Jurassic Park* [1993], which trails by $50 million!)

His visually stunning adaptation of *The Color Purple* (1985), based on the Pulitzer Prize–winning book by Alice Walker, was nominated for best picture, and Oprah Winfrey was nominated for best supporting actress.

Spielberg won an Oscar for best director for the Holocaust drama *Schindler's List*, which the Academy voted best picture of 1993.

Jurassic Park (1993) and *The Lost World: Jurassic Park* (1997) are visually impressive, hi-tech dinosaur stories (set in the 1990s), and they took in hundreds of millions. But be forewarned: They fill audiences with terror (as did *Jaws*) rather than wonder. These are not cute creatures.

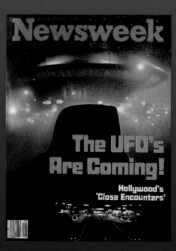

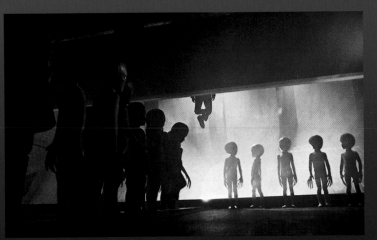

Spielberg's *Close Encounters* is your basic "why won't anyone believe me" story, but is told with a new sensibility. Spielberg's protagonist isn't some doctor, but a joe (far left) who works for the local electrical utility. The film was produced under tight security, which generated much interest before its Christmastime 1977 release. The film's sublime visions crescendo in a 20-minute sequence of total majesty.

Oddly enough, *E.T. The Extra-Terrestrial* owes its existence to Spielberg's having hired the great French director François Truffaut to play a part in *Close Encounters*. While Truffaut was watching this new American master direct scenes with Richard Dreyfuss and the children, he suggested that since Spielberg was so wonderful with kids, he should make a film in which kids starred. Again, Spielberg worked under high security, to deter story lines getting leaked to the press. Its basic premise: What would happen if a space traveler accidentally landed on Earth and was discovered by a group of sympathetic children who find that all the alien wants is to go "home"? Audiences were swept away by the convincing creature and wonderful design; the film was the all-time highest grossing film until *Star Wars* was rereleased in 1997.

As is evident from the box office statistics, sci-fi sequels often do very lucrative business in Hollywood. Other than the *Star Wars* films, three sci-fi series that started out in the late '70s stand out: the *Superman*, *Alien*, and *Star Trek* films.

Kirk Alyn handled the role in *Superman* (1948) and *Atom Man versus Superman* (1950), and George Reeves did so in *Superman and the Mole Men* (1951) and on TV for 104 30-minute episodes of *The Adventures of Superman* beginning in late '52. But it is Christopher Reeve who will be best remembered as Superman, the Man of Steel. Reeve handled the Clark Kent/Superman double-identity story line with more grace, charm, humor, and sex appeal than his predecessors, and his first try (*Superman*, 1978) was hot on the hi-tech heels of the watershed Lucas and Spielberg adventures. For the first time in cinema history, Superman really looked like he was flying. And audiences were delighted.

The 1978 *Superman* introduced Christopher Reeve to the masses. Chosen after an exhaustive search, there doesn't seem to have been anyone better suited (!) to the role. This extraordinary film, conceived on a huge scale, was the last film shot by Geoffrey Unsworth (above left, who also shot *2001*) and directed by Richard Donner (above right).

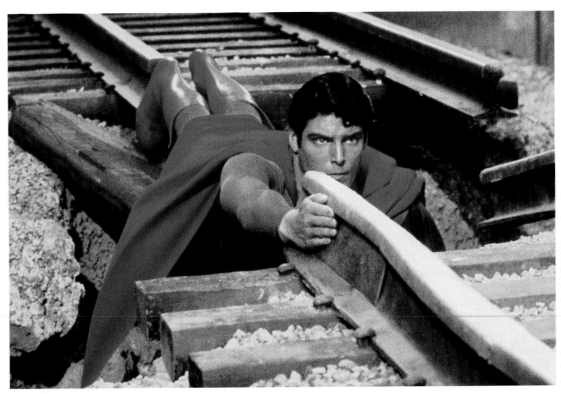

The four *Alien* films—*Alien* (1979), *Aliens* (1986), *Alien³* (1992), and *Alien Resurrection* (1997)—have grossed over $400 million worldwide. *Alien* is equal parts sci-fi and horror: While the crew members of the *Nostromo* spaceship don't particularly like the slimy menace sneaking around outside, John Hurt didn't particularly like having it *inside*. The scene where it bursts forth from his chest cavity has as much impact today as it had decades ago—it is completely unpleasant. Sigourney Weaver's Officer Ripley is the ship's lone survivor; she awakes 57 years later in *Aliens* to save planet LV-425 from alien offspring. She wishes she'd stayed in bed, but audiences are glad she got up because Ripley remains one of filmdom's strongest women characters, and Weaver succeeds at bringing humanity, vulnerability, and fear to a character who can't afford to be anything less than murderous and defensive. It's a great performance.

The story goes as follows: English director Ridley Scott was preparing his second feature—a film of a Wagner opera—when he went to see *Star Wars*. The rest is history. The *Alien* films have now become a franchise for the movie studio that finally said yes to *Star Wars*: 20th Century-Fox.

Alien contains some of the nastiest alien invaders ever conceived. They are the work of the master surrealist, Swiss artist H. R. Giger, whose unsettling paintings inspired Scott to freak out audiences as they'd never been freaked out before. In *Aliens* (1986), at least they gave Ripley some protection!

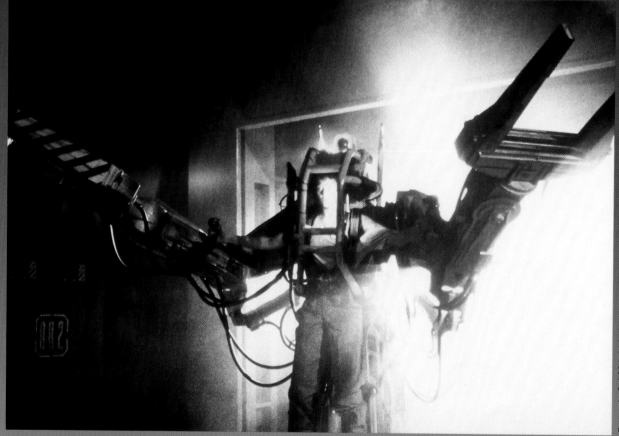

Hollywood has gotten unprecedented mileage out of *Star Trek*. The silver screen saga, which began in 1979 with *Star Trek: The Motion Picture*, is still going strong after eight films. That first one was directed by Robert (*The Day the Earth Stood Still*) Wise, and was well received by Trekkies and critics, while introducing new moviegoers to the *Star Trek* phenomenon. The others were

Star Trek II: The Wrath of Khan (1982)
Star Trek III: The Search for Spock (1984)
Star Trek IV: The Voyage Home (1986)
Star Trek V: The Final Frontier (1989)
Star Trek VI: The Undiscovered Country (1991)
Star Trek: Generations (1994)
Star Trek: First Contact (1996)

The fifth is generally considered the weakest of the lot; *Generations* unites the cast of the original TV series with that of the TV spin-off *Star Trek: The Next Generation*; and *First Contact*, perhaps the most well regarded of all the *Star Trek* films, is the first to do without Captain Kirk (William Shatner) and Mr. Spock (Leonard Nimoy).

CONTACT

$cience Fiction Today

Advances in technology continually change the way movies are made. Once viewers see a sample of what is possible, their expectations are raised, and they will no longer tolerate actors-as-dinosaurs crushing toy cars. Production costs continue to soar, but when viewers are dazzled, so do box office receipts.

In the summer of 1997 alone, *The Lost World: Jurassic Park* (left) took in more than $225 million. Two other major sci-fi films came out that summer: *Contact*, starring Jodie Foster and Matthew McConaughey, was based on Carl Sagan's best-selling novel and topped the $100 million mark; and *Men in Black* (opposite page, top center), which grossed an astronomical $237 million. *Men in Black* starred Will Smith, who was featured in the previous summer's blockbuster *Independence Day* (above, at $306 million). Who knew that a rap-singer-turned-sitcom-actor would go on to star in two of Hollywood's biggest moneymakers?

Futures of the Past

In my pubescent years, three films were released that left a lifelong impression on me. They were tales of the future that filled me with such wonder and delight, and a sense of possibility that I've never lost to this day. Those films were *Metropolis* (1927), *High Treason* (1929), and *Just Imagine* (1930).

Austrian director Fritz Lang's *Metropolis* was the silent screen masterpiece of the soaring stratoscrapers, the capital of the world 100 years hence with its population of 60 million, its videophones, its Robotrix, its humungous man-devouring machinery, its spellbinding splendor. In its time, it was completely revolutionary, on so many levels: The cinematography is as dazzling as and more imaginative than that in most present-day movies; its depiction of the future is in many ways prophetic; and its original length was an epic 182 minutes (this in the days when 90 minutes was considered long). The British two-hour edit is the most commonly available version, though there is a rare American 75-minute version. In 1984, disco record producer Giorgio Moroder issued a restored version of *Metropolis* with a somewhat objectionable rock soundtrack. If you rent it, glory in the images and turn down the sound.

English director Maurice Elvey's *High Treason* (1929) would be a forgotten film but for the fact that I keep it alive. There's a copy in the Cinémathèque de Bruxelles in Belgium and one in the possession of the British Film Institute. Both are silent, although the version I saw repeatedly upon first showing was all-talking. *High Treason*, like *Metropolis*, depicted a videophone, plus a futuristic dining hall with sword-fencing entertainment and

The creators of the brilliant *Metropolis* (1927): Thea von Harbou, who cowrote the screenplay, and Fritz Lang, the film's director. Below, in her first film role, Brigitte Helm has a Robotrix created in her image.

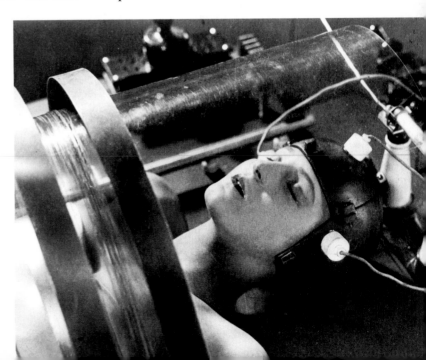

an entire band in the hands of a single musician; an English Channel tunnel decades before it came to be; zeppelins gas-bombing a major American city. It also showed the heroine, played by Benita Hume, taking a shower in a steam-filled stall behind translucent glass, which was rather racy in its day. (Years later, in 1936, a scene would be censored from H. G. Wells's classic *Things to Come* because for a split second it showed a baby boy standing up in a washtub in a war-ruined world with his bare bottom showing!)

Just Imagine (1930) is a musical comedy set in 1980 featuring Maureen O'Sullivan (Johnny Weissmuller's Jane in six *Tarzan* films) as the young heroine LN-18 in a world of indexed numbers. A glorious futuristic city akin to that in *Metropolis* was constructed in a dirigible hangar in a Los Angeles suburb. Mini-monoplanes and

(Opposite page) The London of the 1940s as envisioned in the 1929 British film *High Treason*. It depicts the usual aeroplanes and such, along with 50-story Tudor skyscrapers (notice how insignificant the houses of Parliament are on the left edge of the picture). Publicity materials for this film are impossible to acquire today: This poster was painted from a faded photo I ran across. *Just Imagine* (right) was an all-singing, all-talking, all-futuristic musical set in 1980, starring Maureen O'Sullivan. She's out to prove that happiness is just a warm monoplane! The scene below was reprised in a *Flash Gordon* serial.

aerial traffic cops dot the New York skies. The town is filled with artificial food, drink, and…babies! The one-liner "Give me the good old days!" referred to a 1930s man's preference for the natural way of producing offspring over the 1980 test-tube way, and kept a revival of the film off the screen for many years because of the bluenose of the censorial Hays Office.

Just Imagine climaxed with a rocket trip to Mars and the adventures there with a race of twins, half good, half bad. The rocket itself, I learned a year or two later, was made of papier-mâché and was left to rot by the elements in a deserted lot!

In 1930, as a publicity stunt for *Just Imagine*, a time capsule was sunk under the sidewalk leading to the Carthay Circle Theater in Beverly Hills. It was to be opened in 1980. Alas, by 1980 the famous theater had been razed and tons of concrete covered the location of the time capsule. I suspect I was the only human being on Earth at the time who remembered the buried treasure. Do you suppose it may be discovered centuries hence? *Just imagine!*

(Opposite page) These "miniatures" for *Just Imagine* were almost 25 feet high and were constructed in an aeroplane hangar. (Above) In *Just Imagine*, the costumes were a tour de force. Sophie Wachner was the head wardrobe mistress; she teamed with designers Alice O'Neil and Dolly Tree.

The opening reel of Alexander Korda's production of *Things to Come* (1936), based on H. G. Wells's *The Shape of Things to Come*, depicts the course Britain was to take through World War II and beyond. It just makes one's heart stop, it's so eerie in its predictions. If you haven't hunted this film down, you should—it won't disappoint.

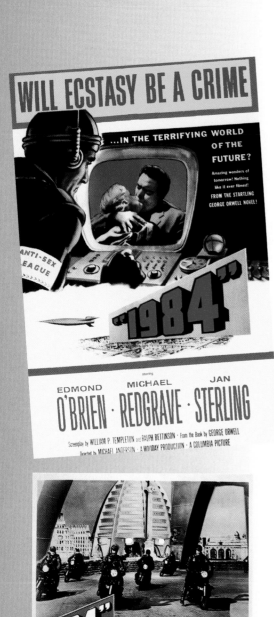

Dystopias

Why have dystopian tales existed throughout the history of science fiction? Perhaps it is because science fiction writers have an admirable sense of social responsibility. They see our present-day troubles—overpopulation, untrustworthy governments, misuse of technological advances, increasing societal desensitization to violence—and they are inspired to thoroughly spell out the worst-case scenario in gruesome detail, so that we think more critically about what it is that we call *progress*.

There have been dozens of dystopias in the history of sci-fi on film: These are but a few that have left the biggest impressions on me.

The 1955 version of *1984*, directed by Michael Anderson, is much better than Michael Radford's 1984 remake, although Radford's is bleaker and arguably closer to the spirit of Orwell's novel. When I originally read the book in 1948, I thought I would rather put a bullet through my brain than live in a world monitored by Big Brother. For me, neither film has attained the power of the written word in Orwell's book—my favorite version, in fact, was the faithful 1954 British TV version featuring a young Peter Cushing.

In *The Time Machine* (1960), a pathetic passive population of the far future is at the mercy of man-eating mutants. George Pal won his fifth special-effects Academy Award for this Wellsian dystopia.

The Tenth Victim (1965) is based on Robert Scheckley's short story "The Seventh Victim." Civilization is dehumanized in the next century and murder is permitted by a cynical government in order to keep population in check and minimize the tendency toward war between nations. Wealth and personal privileges are the reward of "hunters" who achieve "ten-kill."

Fahrenheit 451 (1966) was adapted from the classic Ray Bradbury story of a frightening future in which firemen arrive with gasoline in their hoses (rather than water) as messengers of a book-burning government. Although it was not completely realized to Bradbury's content by the late François Truffaut, it is nevertheless worth repeated viewings. The cinematography by Nicolas Roeg is outstanding.

Wild in the Streets (1968) depicts a New America in which very few present-day Americans would care to live. Half the population is under 25 and "retirement" is almost as bad as in *Logan's Run*: People unlucky enough to live to 35 in this Utopia spend their remaining days on LSD against their will.

(Opposite) The 1955 version of George Orwell's *1984* starred Edmond O'Brien and Jan Sterling. (Right, from top) The future is filled with nasty Morlocks who prey on the civilized ones in *The Time Machine* (1960); Marcello Mastroianni is Italy's *La Decima Vittima (The Tenth Victim)* (1965), in which Ursula Andress hunts and kills men; and Oskar Werner and Julie Christie in François Truffaut's film version of *Fahrenheit 451* (1966).

Stanley Kubrick's *A Clockwork Orange* (1971) ran into censorship trouble in the land of its birth; in fact, I believe it is banned to this day in Old Blighty. It received three Oscar nominations (including best picture, best director, and best film editing) but didn't win in any categories; however, it was voted Best Film of the Year by the New York Film Critics. The ultraviolence and hallucinogenic drugs got to my guts and convinced me more than ever that I'm glad I've led a drug-free life. But I loved the future slang (didn't you, *droogie?*), as I myself have had a habit of coining terms (as in *This scientifilm is a cinemadaptation of Anthony Burgess's popular novel*).

THX 1138 (1971) gave us the first glimpse of George Lucas as a science fiction filmmaker. It depicts a sterile underground black-and-white future run by machines against which Robert Duvall rebels. The ideas aren't highly original—love is prohibited as in *1984*; folks have numbers for names as in *Just Imagine*; technology malfunctions and disaster ensues as in countless sci-fi parables. But it is a fun, worthwhile renter from the director who went on to give us *Star Wars*.

In Max Ehrlich's screenplay for *Z.P.G. (Zero Population Growth)* (1972), we see an overpopulated society of the future in which it is verboten for anyone to have children for the next 30 years. A young couple doesn't agree with the government and defies the law by having a baby. Not a very wise thing to do.

Soylent Green (1973) is a winner based on Harry Harrison's *Make Room! Make Room!* This was the last role for Edward G. Robinson—his death scene was all-the-more poignant by the fact that he was actually dying. Society is perspiring and overpopulated in 2022 and food is in short supply. Charlton Heston makes the staggering discovery that the artificial food known as soylent green is actually...*dead human flesh!* One of the best dystopian films.

In the 21st-century world of *Rollerball* (1975), individual nations have been replaced by worldwide corporations intent on zombifying the masses by involving them in futuristic Roman circus games played to the death on skates.

Death Race 2000 (1975), an Ib Melchior story, featured an early appearance by Sylvester Stallone. "In the year 2000, hit and run driving is no longer a felony, it's the national sport!"

In *Logan's Run* (1976), two centuries hence, life doesn't begin at 40, it ends for most at 30. But some 30-year-olds aren't content to call it quits so soon, and Michael York's task is to run 'em down and eliminate them. Outside the domed (doomed) civilization, an old man is discovered, which proves longevity can be achieved.

In *Escape from New York* (1981), director John Carpenter's Manhattan is, in 1997, a violence-wracked prison island on which the president's plane crash-lands! A dark vision that fortunately didn't eventuate.

Blade Runner (1982), cinemadapted from Philip K. Dick's "Do Androids Dream of Electric Sheep?," has become a modern classic. In this futuristic police melodrama, Harrison Ford has the task of trying to track down renegade androids in a metropolis gone mad. The broiling, neon-dominated city is amazing, and the interior of the 100-year-old Bradbury Building (a

(Opposite page, top of bottom) Malcolm McDowell as the leader of a gang of vicious street thugs in Kubrick's *A Clockwork Orange* (1971); one of the silver-faced police androids from George Lucas's *THX 1138* (1971); and the riot police sweeping up the extras in *Soylent Green* (1973). (Above) The wonderful *Death Race 2000* (1975) with David Carradine.

Ridley Scott turned a Philip K. Dick story into the elaborate, moody *Blade Runner*. In what was to become the granddaddy of dystopian futures, Scott and company suggested that L.A. in 2019 would be overrun with oil fields, tall buildings with videos projected on their sides, and lots of dirt. Shunned by the general public the year *E.T.* came out, the letterbox laserdisc released by Voyager kept the film alive until Warner Bros. decided to yield to pressure and release the director's version without Harrison Ford's intrusive narration, which was added at the studio's insistence just prior to the film's original release.

triumph of architecture designed by my maternal grandfather) is brilliantly incorporated and serves the plot well.

Terry Gilliam's *Brazil* (1985) was not to my liking, but this nightmarish depiction of an Orwellian government has its fans. Gilliam's *12 Monkeys* (1995) is a far more engrossing story—a time-travel tale in which one of the few survivors of a deadly virus travels back in time to prevent the death of man. Brad Pitt received a best supporting actor Oscar nomination.

Terry Gilliam is one of today's most eccentric filmmakers. His visions of a dystopian future seem, with each passing film, to be taking place in the same dysfunctional world. The paperwork-obsessed bureaucrats and socialities who pester Jonathan Pryce in *Brazil* (above) also torment Bruce Willis in *12 Monkeys* (opposite).

Atomigeddon

In a ploy that would later be used in hundreds of student films and television commercials, director Ranald MacDougall got everybody up super early to film Harry Belafonte (as the last man on Earth) wander around a deserted Manhattan in *The World, the Flesh, and the Devil* (1959). Don't worry, he'll eventually run into Inger Stevens (the last bombshell on Earth).

The earliest after-the-bomb film was seen in 1951 but had its origin 13 years earlier in a radio play called *The Word* starring none other than Bette Davis! The original radio version was a two-character drama about the last couple on Earth. After the advent of the atomic bomb, author Arch Oboler added the nuclear element and three more characters and changed its name to *Five*. Five survivors of an Earthwide nuclear nightmare degenerate, plagued by racism and jealousy for the possession of the last woman on Earth. The advertising campaign told the story succinctly:

One—One girl.

Two—Two hours of the most spellbinding entertainment ever filmed.

Three—A story of the three elemental passions: love, hate, fear!

Four—Four men alone with the knowledge that in all the world there is only one woman!

FIVE!

The theme was revisited in 1959, when the world's populace was reduced to three in *The World, the Flesh, and the Devil,* a cinemadaptation of M. P. Shiel's incredible novel, *The Purple Cloud.* Mel Ferrer, as a white racist male, was pitted against Harry Belafonte for the affection of Inger Stevens in an eerily empty New York City. And the next year, two men were at it again, fighting over *The Last Woman on Earth*; Robert Towne wrote the screenplay and was one of the two men.

Of the nuclear-age monster films, two are particularly memorable. In *World Without End* (1955), monster men dominate the surface of a nuclear-ruined world, terrorizing underground survivors of civilization who suffer from anemia. And Roger Corman's *The Day the World Ended* (1956) is about atomic war survivors who face mutant monsters, including a three-eyed scaly humanoid known as the Cucumber Creature.

On a more intellectual note, three of the smarter atom bomb–oriented films are *On the Beach* (1959) with Gregory Peck, Ava Gardner, Anthony Perkins, and Fred Astaire; Stanley Kubrick's black comedy *Dr. Strangelove, or How I Learned to Stop Worrying and Love the Bomb* (1964), for which Peter Sellers received an Oscar nomination for his portrayal of three different men; and *Testament* (1983), for which Jane Alexander received a nomination as well.

Finally, on a more kinky note, *A Boy and His Dog* (1975) is a downbeat story of a young man and his telepathic canine companion in a nuclear-devastated wasteland. Man's Best Friend is starving when they come upon a girl. The hero sacrifices his desire for a sexual companion for the hunger pangs of his four-legged friend. The hackle-raising climax may be summarized in six words: Boy Meets Girl, Dog Eats Girl.

"You can't fight in here, this is the War Room!" is only one of the famous lines from Stanley Kubrick's *Dr. Strangelove, or How I Learned to Stop Worrying and Love the Bomb* (1964). Audience members left the film imitating the telephone exchange between Peter Sellers as the U.S. president (below, right) and the Soviet premier, while Peter Bull as the Soviet ambassador (below, left) listens in: "Yes, Dmitri. I'm calling about the bomb. Yes—the *atomic* bomb, Dmitri…."

Copyright © 1963 by Columbia Pictures

Brain New World

How can you tell if your mates have had their brains stolen by aliens? They spend a lot of time holding their hands to their foreheads. Below, Marshall Thompson demonstrates in *Fiend Without a Face* (1958). Opposite, Boris does it best in *The Man Who Lived Again* (1936).

And there's Joyce Meadows discovering that it's no use, they will come to get her, too, as she finds the sheriff has been taken over by *The Brain from Planet Arous* (1958).

Considering the function of the brain, you would think that brain movies would be some of the genre's more philosophical, thought-provoking, and creative endeavors. Well, think again! Most brain movies are pure camp and quite gooey. There are a number of worthwhile films that stand out, however, and I hope you'll use this as a quick-reference guide to help you avoid the tripe.

The Man Who Lived Again (1936) features Karloff in one of his best!

The Brain Eaters (1958) is noteworthy because Robert Heinlein sued for uncredited adaptation of his *Puppet Masters* (which eventually reached the screen under its own title in 1994). A pre-Spock appearance of Leonard Nimoy will be of interest to *Star Trek* fanatics.

There were two somewhat silly brain films in 1958: *The Brain from Planet Arous* gave actor John Agar a bad time as it strove to seduce his girlfriend and incidentally conquer the world. And *Fiend Without a Face*, based on Amelia Reynolds Long's 1930 weird-science short story "The Thought-Monster," featured naked flying brains in its finale. To counter such exotica, *The Space Children* came out that same year and featured, finally, a benevolent space brain that arrives on Earth to nullify the atomic weapons race.

But the best of the brain movies are definitely those based on Curt Siodmak's *Donovan's Brain*. It has been filmed no less than three times, the first featuring Erich von Stroheim, billed in his heyday as "The Man You Love to Hate," in the film known as *The Lady and the Monster* (1944). The plot concerns a scientist who comes across a plane-crash victim whose body is irreparable but whose brain is not dead. He removes the brain and stores it in a glass container of liquid in his laboratory. Donovan's brain develops telepathic powers and eventually takes control of the lab assistant, making him his mental slave. In the 1953 version, the only one actually called *Donovan's Brain*, the disembodied brain of a tycoon (Donovan) takes over a brain scientist named Dr. Cory and bends Cory's will to perform the tycoon's evil bidding. The late Lew Ayres played the experimenter this time around and his leading lady was none other than Nancy Davis (Reagan)! The final version (1962), jointly known as *The Brain* and *Vengeance*, was a British/German collaboration starring Peter Van Eyck as the surgeon (now Dr. *Corry*), whose brain is periodically taken over by the living dead man now known as Max Holt. Holt's passion is to use Corry to play detective and determine who was responsible for his "death." A sequel (never produced) was suggested at the climax, as in this version the brain was

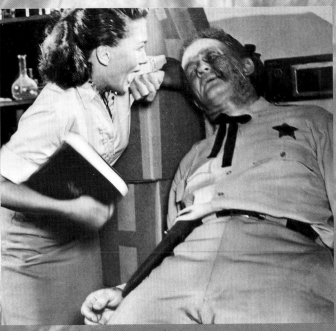

One of the greatest films of the early sound era is *King Kong* (1933), the wild brainchild of directors Merian C. Cooper and Ernest B. Schoedsack. The two men convinced RKO executive David O. Selznick to fund the project. Everyone in Hollywood thought they were nuts. Nothing like this had ever been attempted, but it defined the style of the monster picture, influencing almost every monster pic to come. Below, filmmaker Carl Denham (played by Robert Armstrong) films Ann Darrow (played by Fay Wray) in a rehearsal prior to landing at Skull Island, where there is a rumor of a giant ape. Denham and his crew have many adventures tracking down the beast, and finally bring him down in New York.

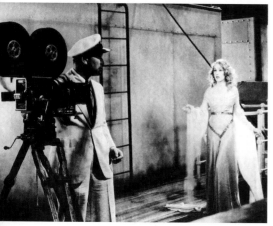

not destroyed but continued to dominate its savior. Some years ago in an annual fantasy film festival in Sitges, Spain, I saw a Russian sci-fi flick called *Professor Dowell's Head* adapted from the novel of the same name by Alexander Beliaev. Siodmak was given no credit, but the story was a Soviet-styled but otherwise identical version of *Donovan's Brain*.

Carl Reiner's *The Man with Two Brains* (1983) starring Steve Martin and Kathleen Turner is a delightful spoof: Martin lusts after Turner's body but loves another woman's mind. You can guess how he solves his problem.

Giant Stars of Sci-Fi Films: Dinosaurs, Apes, and Reptiles

Willis H. O'Brien was a special-effects technician who won an Oscar for his work on 1949's gorilla story, *Mighty Joe Young*. But his first project, some 32 years earlier, was *The Dinosaur and the Missing Link*, a one-reel Edison short of 1914. O'Brien himself was seen in *The Ghost of Slumber Mountain* (1918), another short with animated dinosaurs. Then in 1925, O'Brien animated 49 prehistoric creatures (including a pterodactyl that is now in my collection) built by Marcel Delgado for the cinemadaptation of Sir Arthur Conan Doyle's *The Lost World*. O'Brien's craft again dazzled audiences for director Merian C. Cooper's giant-ape masterpiece, *King Kong*, in 1933. (I purchased the model of the pteranodon that was trying to fly away with Fay Wray from the brother of the late Rod Serling.)

To my chagrin, Dino De Laurentiis produced the

"THE MOST AWESOME THRILLER OF ALL TIME"

the one and only

KING KONG

with
FAY WRAY
ROBT. ARMSTRONG
BRUCE CABOT

A
MERIAN C. COOPER –
ERNEST B. SCHOEDSACK
PRODUCTION

FROM A STORY BY
EDGAR WALLACE
AND
MERIAN C. COOPER

Chief Technician
WILLIS J. O'BRIEN

DAVID O. SELZNICK
Executive Producer

"Don't worry, ladies and gentlemen, those chains are made of chromium steel...." Well, Kong, like Houdini, would not be restrained. Cooper and Schoedsack knew what they were doing by letting Kong climb to the top of the newly completed Empire State Building—it made for one of the most incredible sequences in movie history.

1976 *King Kong* but left out the dinosaurs altogether. Dinosaurs were an integral part of the original *Kong*; the dino-less remake was tantamount to making *The Jolson Story* without Al singing or *The Astaire Story* without Fred dancing!

The Japanese introduced us to their own King Kong in the 1954 *Godzilla, King of the Monsters*. The 400-foot Godzilla (or Gojira in Japan) differed from other gargantuan beings of the silver-screen (such as Kong, Mighty Joe Young, and the Ymir) in that he was played by a man in a suit rather than some miniature metal model animated by Willis H. O'Brien or Ray Harryhausen. Godzilla is a hibernating reptile brought out of slumber by the explosion of an atomic bomb; he started out ravaging the Nipponese countryside but through a dozen or more incarnations metamorphosed

The *Jurassic Park* films contain by far the most grotesque and most believable dinosaurs yet seen on screen. Although both films have been megahits, neither contain characters that have been particularly embraced by the public. Jeff Goldblum (below) is the only actor to appear in both films. The dinosaurs are definitely the stars here. When word got out that Spielberg's sequel would be called *The Lost World: Jurassic Park*, I mistakenly presumed that the master director was adapting Sir Arthur Conan Doyle's classic dinosaur story. Similarly, I had hoped his mid-'80s TV series, *Steven Spielberg's Amazing Stories*, would bring to the screen classic (and long-forgotten) tales from the pulp magazine *Amazing Stories*.

Copyright © 1997 by Universal Studios Inc. and Amblin Entertainment, Inc.

from a people-and-building pulverizer into a heroic figure. Godzilla spawned a number of imitators and competitors, including Atragon, Biollante, Gaigan, Gamera, Ghidrah, Gigantis, Mechagodzilla, Megalon, Monster

Zero, Mothra, the Sea Monster, the Smog Monster, and
the Thing. He even fought King Kong—lost to him in
America, bested him in Japan.

Are bullets any use against atomic mutant ants? James Whitmore and Joan Weldom take a shot at it in *Them!* (1954). (Opposite page) The ultimate in insectales: *The Fly*. In the 1958 version (top), David Hedison, under wraps to conceal the fact that he's turning into a mutant, shows the controls to his matter transporter to a skeptical Patricia Owens. In director David Cronenberg's 1986 remake, Jeff Goldblum is about to peel off his fingernails—in close-up.

Insects

Them!, in which atomic testing inadvertently yields "gi-ants," was Warner Bros.' most successful movie in

Copyright © 1954 by Warner Bros. Pictures

1954. The bugs are supposedly exterminated by poison gas, but what happened to the eggs of the queen bug? This is *the* classic bug movie!

Tarantula (1955) and *The Incredible Shrinking Man* (1957), both directed by Jack Arnold, feature giant spiders, which are arguably more frightening than giant ants. In the former, cattle, people, and cars are victims of a spider that's been fed special nutrients. In the latter, written by Hugo Award recipient Richard Matheson, exposure to radiation shrinks the leading man down to less than an inch; he has close encounters with not only the hairy arachnid but also the family cat.

In Kurt Neumann's *The Fly* (1958), a researcher builds a matter transporter in which his own matter is unwittingly mixed with that of a common household fly. (Director David Cronenberg did a remake in 1986 that sticks close to the original story but is a lot gorier. Both will leave you bug-eyed.)

Invisibility

In 1898, H. G. Wells published *The Invisible Man*, and since the dawn of cinema it's inspired many a filmmaker.

For instance, in a Biograph silent short of 1908, *The Invisible Fluid*, a scientist has perfected a liquid that, when sprayed from an atomizer, causes 10-minute stretches of invisibility. The atomizer gets into the hands of a young prankster who, among other things, leaves a bride screaming by "deleting" her bridegroom. After his nonviolent crime spree ends, he is caught by the authorities, who hold the atomizer as evidence. The kid is asked to demonstrate his implausible story in court; once he regains control of the atomizer, he simply disappears and escapes.

The 1910 French short *L'Homme Invisible* (*An Invisible Thief*) begins with a shot of the Wells novel. This time, the lead character drinks the potion and becomes a menace rather than a prankster. He robs a house and then a couple, and terrorizes the police who are stalking him.

In 1923, Henry B. Walthall (the legendary Little Colonel of 1915's *The Birth of a Nation*) starred in *The Unknown Purple* as a scientist who'd been unjustly sentenced to prison. He creates, upon his release, a violet light that renders him invisible, giving him the ability to wreak havoc on those who betrayed him.

In 1933, Universal introduced Claude Rains in the all-time invisibility classic—James Whale's *The Invisible Man*. Some 60 years later, at a convention in Crystal City, Virginia—in the presence of such notables as Ray Bradbury, Robert Bloch, Curt Siodmak, Richard Matheson, Ann Robinson, William Schallert, Joe Dante, John Landis, and dozens more—I had the honor of

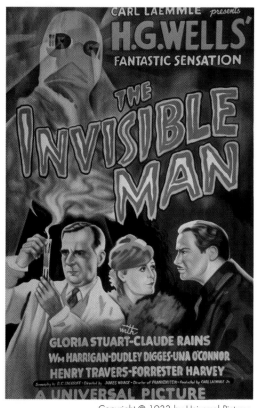

Copyright © 1933 by Universal Pictures

sitting opposite the female star of *The Invisible Man*, glorious Gloria Stuart, and read Rains's part from one of their scenes to the best of my ability. It was one of the highlights of my life. Gloria flattered me by saying, "Forry, you did it better than Mr. Rains." No, Gloria, no; not in a thousand years; but I love you for thinking so.

Sequels included *The Invisible Man Returns* (1940), *Invisible Agent* (1942), and *The Invisible Man's Revenge* (1944)—there was even *Abbott and Costello Meet the Invisible Man* (1951). There was the inevitable *Invisible Woman* (Virginia Bruce, 1941) with John Barrymore. And filmmakers in Germany, Japan, Mexico, and Turkey created their own invisible men. Mr. Wells, what you wrought!

Dr. Jekyll & Mr. Hyde

Robert Louis Stevenson's tale of the experimenter attempting to chemically separate man's dark side from his light, with disastrous results, has served as one of the most oft-filmed sci-fi stories of all time. Between 1908 and 1925 there were no less than a dozen versions. The best-remembered and most popular featured the matinee idol of the day, John Barrymore ("the Great Profile"), who effected the change from Jekyll to Hyde without makeup in 1920! In another 1920 movie, Conrad Veidt (as Dr. Warren and Mr. O'Connor) and Bela Lugosi (!) starred in a German variation known as *Der Januskopf* (*Janus-Faced*). One of the most unusual versions was comedic: *Dr. Pickle and Mr. Pride* (1925), featuring none other than Stan Laurel in his pre–Laurel and Hardy days! Rouben Mamoulian's 1932

The incomparable John Barrymore in the 1920 version of *Dr. Jekyll and Mr. Hyde*.

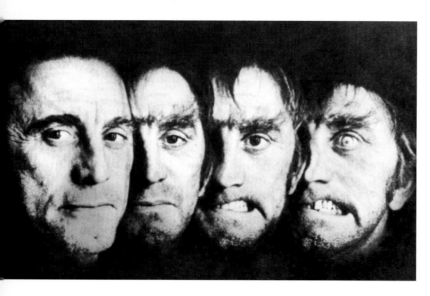

Songs about debauchery, anyone? They had 'em in the made-for-TV version of *Dr. Jekyll and Mr. Hyde* (1973), starring Kirk Douglas (above). The best version is the one directed by Rouben Mamoulian (1932) starring that year's best actor Oscar recipient, Fredric March, who looks good wearing evening clothes, but when he drinks that serum, watch out!

version earned Fredric March his first of two Academy Awards. The story was filmed again in 1941 with Spencer Tracy, Ingrid Bergman, and Lana Turner. Kirk Douglas and Michael Redgrave starred in an ill-conceived musical version made for TV in 1973, and in a 1976 blaxploitation version, *Dr. Black and Mr. Hyde,* Dr. Black becomes a white-skinned monster. Tim Daly, from TV's *Wings,* starred in the box-office flop *Dr. Jekyll and Ms. Hyde* (1995), in which estrogen gets added to his famous potion; predictable inanity follows. Through the years, it seems as if Dr. Jekyll has had nowhere to Hyde!

Robots

The grandest robot of all time was created in 1927 for Fritz Lang's *Metropolis* by Walter Schultze-Mittendorf, who recreated her toward the end of his life for the Cinémathèque in Paris (the original no longer exists). He gave the new Robotrix a back that originally did not exist. So when I had my replica built—by Bill Malone and Oscar-winner Bob Short over a period of a year and a half and 600 hours—I had my own back created for her, based on the naked back of a nudist I had admired in the camp I frequented for several years. I christened her Ultima Futura Automaton, after the initials of UFA, the studio (Universum Film Aktiengessellschaft: Universe Film Association) that produced her.

Besides the *Metropolis* robot, the other most famous ones are Gort from *The Day The Earth Stood Still* and Robby from *Forbidden Planet*. The actual robot from *Tobor the Great* (Get it? Robot spelled backwards) was in front of a shop on Beverly Boulevard only a couple of hours before it was stolen.

Karel Čapek, the Czech author who had the good fortune to die shortly before Hitler would have eliminated him, gave the world the term *robot* (Czech for "worker") in the famous play *R.U.R. Rossum's Universal Robots*. (*Rossum* is the Czech word for "brain.") Oddly, the robots of Čapek's play were flesh and blood creations that today are more commonly called androids; robots in movies principally refer to mechanical creations in humanoid form. I find it amazing that *R.U.R.* was never filmed. Below, Robby the Robot takes control in *Forbidden Planet* (1956).

A rogues' gallery of robots:
Top left, *The Colossus of
New York* (1958); above,
Robby the Robot from
Forbidden Planet (1956);
left, *Tobor the Great*
(1954). (Opposite page)
A scene from *Logan's Run*
(1976), and Bruce Dern
with one of the drones from
Silent Running (1971).

FJA SINGS "RO-RO-RO YOUR BOT"

FAVORITE ALL-TIME ROBOTS

The faux Maria in
Metropolis (1927)

The slave robots of Murania
in *The Phantom Empire*
(1935), starring Gene
Autry (!)

Gort in *The Day the Earth
Stood Still* (1951)

Chani in *Devil Girl from
Mars* (1954)

Gog and Magog in the 3-D
Gog (1954)

Death ray–equipped robots in
Target Earth (1954)

Tobor the Great (1954)

The Colossus of New York
(1958), a robot with a
transplanted human brain

Huey, Dewey, and Louie,
some of the kinder robots,
played by legless actors in
Silent Running (1971)

Maximilian in *The Black
Hole* (1979), the villain's
henchman, designed to
look like the Demon in
Disney's *Fantasia*

CHAPTER FIVE
Sci-Fi
on Television

Television has not produced as many sci-fi classics as one might expect. Whereas pulps such as *Argosy* were around in the late 1800s and have since produced thousands of stories, and hundreds of films have been made throughout the 20th century, television is relatively young. Though there were televised events as early as the '20s, it wasn't until the early '50s that TV sets penetrated a large percentage of American households. Here, then, is a review not of all sci-fi that has hit the airwaves but rather those that have made a significant contribution to the genre.

THE TWILIGHT ZONE

"There is a fifth dimension beyond that which is known to man. It is a dimension vast as space and timeless as infinity. It is the middle ground between light and shadow, between the pit of his fears and the summit of his knowledge. This is the dimension of imagination. It is an area we call *The Twilight Zone.*" Thus were awestruck viewers introduced to Rod Serling—creator, executive producer, host, narrator, and prolific writer extraordinaire—in 1959. By 1963 he had delivered more than 150 awesome episodes; most would fall into the fantasy category, but many certainly crossed over into the world of science fiction.

"Time Enough at Last" was based on a story by my client Lyn Venable; the late Burgess Meredith starred as the last man in New York after a nuclear attack, content that he could now gorge himself on good literature in the public library without pesky

The Twilight Zone is a cultural phenomenon. Everyone, young and old, has seen at least some of these shows. Top, Antoinette Bower and Richard Basehart as Adam and Eve in "Probe 7—Over and Out"; above, Jonathan Winters goads Jack Klugman in "A Game of Pool"; right, John Hoyt listens as Inger Stevens explains it all in "The Lateness of the Hour."

The *Twilight Zone* episodes sometimes had some pretty big names appearing in them, and the women who suffered along with them, well, who knows? (Top) Lee Marvin is cautious about taking a drink offered by Ellen Willard in an episode called "From Beyond the Grave." (Bottom) Roddy McDowall and Susan Oliver in the Mars story "People Are Alike All Over."

interruptions. . . until he, an extreme myopic, drops and breaks his only pair of glasses!

There were more than a dozen Richard Matheson stories, including space-travel tales such as "And When the Sky Was Opened," "Third from the Sun," and "The Invaders" (with Agnes Moorehead); time-travel tales such as "The Last Flight" and "Once Upon a Time," featuring Buster Keaton as a janitor who finds himself 72 years in the future; a robot story, "Steel," starring Lee Marvin; and the classic starring a young William Shatner, "Nightmare at 20,000 Feet."

Ray Bradbury wrote "I Sing the Body Electric" about an android grandmother.

Serling himself scripted more than 80 episodes. Many of them were strong fantasy stories about paranormal phenomena such as telepathy, parallel dimensions, and premonitions; and many were psychologically oriented, revolving around concepts such as paranoia, wish fulfillment, and repressed memories. But he had a definite tendency toward solid science fiction as well, much of it space related. "The Long Morrow," for instance, is about an astronaut's antiaging device; he also wrote the Martian tales "People Are Alike All Over" and "Will the Real Martian Please Stand Up?"; "The Midnight Sun" (in which an out-of-orbit Earth is plunging into the brightest star); "The Gift" (in which humans kill a visitor from space who was about to offer them a cure for cancer); and "On Thursday We Leave for Home" (with James Whitmore reluctant to leave his asteroid abode for Earth).

The Twilight Zone is also known for casting many up-and-coming TV and film stars (e.g., Bill Bixby, Charles Bronson, Carol Burnett, *The*

Young and the Restless's Jeanne Cooper, Robert Duvall, Peter Falk, Jack Klugman, Ted Knight, Martin Landau, Cloris Leachman, *General Hospital*'s Emily McLaughlin, *Lost in Space*'s Billy Mumy, Leonard Nimoy, Robert Redford, and Burt Reynolds), as well as veterans such as Buster Keaton and Mickey Rooney. Reruns have aired for decades, and the show ages well, as have many of those fine actors.

THE OUTER LIMITS

One might be tempted to call *The Outer Limits* a poor man's *Twilight Zone*. But it never was inferior. And it was definitely scarier, given its predeliction toward bugs, bees, slimy alien creatures, and the like. It aired 49 episodes from 1963 to 1965; my friend Joseph Stefano (who adapted Robert Bloch's novel *Psycho* for the 1960 Hitchcock film) was the producer for the first season's 32 episodes.

A number of teleplays were adapted from works of noted science fiction writers—for example, David Duncan's "The Immortals" (from the October 1960 *Galaxy Magazine*) and "The Human Factor"; Harlan Ellison's "Soldier" and "Demon with a Glass Hand" (both Hugo Award winners); Clifford Simak's "The Duplicate Man"; and Jerry Sohl's "The Invisible Enemy."

Of note to *Star Trek* fans: The adaptation of Otto Binder's "I, Robot" (from the January 1939 issue of *Amazing Stories*) featured Leonard Nimoy. And "Cold Hands, Warm Heart" featured William Shatner as an astronaut whose body and mind are traumatized after a flight to Venus.

The Jetsons was one of the more popular animated sci-fi shows. George Jetson and family rarely encountered dangers—this show was a sitcom, with clever depictions of a space-age future (robot maids and midair traffic jams).

(Above) Part of the legendary crew of the starship *Enterprise* (clockwise from upper left): Nichelle Nichols as Lieutenant Uhura, DeForest Kelley as "Bones" McCoy, William Shatner as Captain Kirk, and Leonard Nimoy as Mr. Spock. (Opposite) Kirk and Spock defend themselves with phasers as they carry out yet another mission to boldly go where no man has gone before.

STAR TREK

Star Trek is one of television's true phenomena. What began in 1966 as a three-season, moderately successful program on NBC has become a perpetually syndicated sci-fi classic that has spawned three TV spin-offs and more than half a dozen Hollywood blockbusters, not to mention cartoons, conventions, and websites.

Star Trek is truly a child of the '60s. As space exploration was accelerated by fierce competition between the United States and the Soviet Union, interest in space among the masses had never been so genuine. It was also a revolutionary period in American history: Civil rights, women's rights, and sexual liberation were changing the mores of the culture, and Gene Roddenberry, the show's creator and producer, assembled a crew for the *Enterprise* that reflected these changes. Mr. Spock, Captain Kirk's first officer, was no simple white guy: He was part human and part Vulcan. The head of communications was an African American *woman*; the starship's navigators were Russian and Japanese. This sense of brotherhood, on an episode-by-episode basis, may have seemed secondary to some of the save-the-universe plots, but it is really the series' foundation.

The writing was also crucial to the show's longevity. Some of sci-fi's most noted writers—Richard Matheson, Robert Bloch, Theodore Sturgeon, Harlan Ellison— wrote for the original series between 1966 and 1969.

Ten years after its last episode, *Star Trek* hit the big screen. Between 1979 and 1986, there were four *Star*

(Above) The crew would often find beautiful aliens in their adventures. Although it was usually Kirk who won their hearts, this one showed a definite preference for Mr. Spock. (Below left) Look out! The *Enterprise* approaches an amoeba-like organism living in space. (Below right) Spock encounters beings who have recreated Earth's ancient Roman civilization on their own planet. (Opposite page top) An annoyed Kirk contemplates the lovable but ubiquitous tribbles whose speedy reproduction cycle causes them to overrun his ship. (Opposite page bottom) The Roman motif revisited.

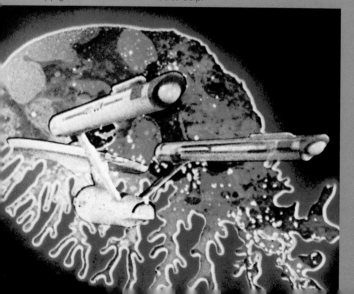

Trek films—all were successful and all starred the same cast as the NBC series. Then, in 1987, Roddenberry created *Star Trek: The Next Generation*, which a number of purist Trekkers were not looking forward to. Why mess with a perfect formula? But *The Next Generation* proved to be an immediate success and gave Roddenberry the opportunity to go hi-tech on TV. However innovative and influential the original *Star Trek* series was, it definitely looks dated and a bit kitschy. *The Next Generation* carried on for seven successful seasons in syndication, during which time the original *Enterprise* crew was featured in two more *Star Trek* movies. In 1994, a Spockless union of the old and new crews was the premise of the film *Star Trek: Generations*.

Star Trek: Deep Space Nine and *Star Trek: Voyager* are the two '90s shows, and their popularity is nowhere near waning. The *Deep Space Nine* ship, the *Defiant*, discovers a hole in space that serves as a high-speed tunnel to uncharted galaxies. The *Voyager* is essentially lost in space and looking for a way home. *Voyager* began two years after *Deep Space Nine*; these are the first of the *Star Trek* shows to be in production simultaneously.

IRWIN ALLEN

Were it not for the *Star Trek* phenomena, sci-fi on TV in the '60s would belong to creator/producer Irwin Allen. In 1964, he brought the submarine *Seaview* into America's homes on a weekly basis—it battled worldly enemies (other countries), other-worldly enemies (aliens), and under-worldly enemies (aquatic creatures) and was always triumphant. The show was *Voyage to the Bottom of the Sea*, and it was based on his 1961 like-titled film. More than 100 episodes of the show were aired.

Lost in Space debuted in 1965 and, like the original *Star Trek*, lasted for only three seasons, but because it has been rerun in syndication for three decades now, it's left a large impression on the popular culture. It's a family show: Husband and wife John and Maureen Robinson are flying around the galaxies with their kids Judy, Penny, and Will, plus a sexy copilot (Major Don West), an embarrassingly lo-tech albeit lovable robot (Robot), and the stowaway saboteur (Dr. Smith). The starship *Jupiter 2* is off course and week after week they try to get closer to home but find themselves confronted by obstacles (outer-space weather conditions, evil extraterrestrials, fuel shortages).

In 1966, with *Voyage* and *Lost* still going strong, Allen gave us *The Time Tunnel*. This one lasted only 30 episodes, but in that short time, its heroes time-traveled to the *Titanic*, Pearl Harbor, the war of 1812, the Trojan war, Custer's last stand, the Alamo, and Gettysburg, and visited with the likes of Marie Antoinette, Robin Hood, the ghost of Nero, Cortez the

Richard Basehart (shown below with guest star Victor Buono) played a stern submarine captain in Irwin Allen's *Voyage to the Bottom of the Sea* (which a *Mad* magazine parody once called *Voyage to See What's on the Bottom!*). Below them, Deanna Lund, a series regular on *Land of the Giants*, struggles against a giant entomologist played by guest star Don Watters.

My Favorite Martian starred the late Bill Bixby and Ray Walston, shown here with guest star Marlo Thomas.

(Opposite page) Clockwise from upper left: Gregory Harrison and Heather Menzies in *Logan's Run*; Belinda J. Montgomery in the wetsuit, and Patrick Duffy, who doesn't need one, in *The Man From Atlantis*; and the cast from *Battlestar Galactica*.

in *The Courtship of Eddie's Father*, a poignant sitcom about a widower and his son, and later played Dr. David Banner in *The Incredible Hulk* series and in a trio of *Hulk* TV movies.

THE 1970s

Science fiction, which fared so well on the big screen in the '70s, did not do so well on television. Two of the more successful shows—*The Six Million Dollar Man* (based on Martin Caidin's novel *Cyborg*) and its spin-off, *The Bionic Woman*—were entertaining, popular, and relatively tepid.

Colonel Steve Austin is a NASA pilot who loses three limbs and an eye in a plane wreck; he gets rebuilt at a cost of (you guessed it!) $6 million, and works as a crimestopper for a government agency. His nuclear-powered replacement parts turn him into a '70s Superman, but the show lacks the humor and the Lois Lane/double-identity subplots of *Superman* and becomes more of a crime drama (though Austin's background in astronautics does bring us out to space once in a while). The show had a remarkable five-season run beginning in 1974.

In *The Bionic Woman*, which first aired in 1976, Jaime Somers gets revived after a fatal accident. She's rebuilt in the same general fashion as Colonel Austin but is also equipped with a bionic ear, so she can listen in on faraway conversations. This one lasted for three seasons and has aged even less gracefully than *The Six Million Dollar Man*. Her slow-motion leaps and gymnastic skills look silly; despite Jaime's nuclear-powered legs, she'd be no match for the non-bionic Buffy (yes, the vampire slayer).

By today's standards, these shows look obviously lo-tech, even though some older sci-fi shows, when held up to the same standards, don't seem dated at all. *The Twilight Zone*, for instance, still has punch because it

relies on imagination and suspense rather than hi-tech trickery. And *Star Trek* so succeeded in creating its own world full of progressive ideas (even if that world has velour and shades of orange not to be found outside of the 1960s) that viewers just go with it. The bionic couple, on the other hand, entertained but contributed nothing significant to the genre.

In 1977, *Logan's Run* debuted, based on the film of the same name, but it lasted merely 14 episodes. It introduced audiences to a pre–sex symbol Gregory Harrison (who went on to star in TV's *Trapper John, M.D.*, the made-for-TV beefcake film *For Ladies Only*, and Broadway's recent Kander and Ebb musical, *Steel Pier*). He plays Logan 5, a 23rd-century cop looking for Sanctuary, a Shangri-la of sorts to which those approaching 30 must flee in order to survive extermination on their 30th birthday, or Lastday.

That same year, *The Man From Atlantis* had a brief life (or quick death) as well. *Dallas*'s Patrick Duffy starred as a survivor of Atlantis who is saved by an attractive woman doctor. They team up for the Foundation of Oceanic Research: His special underwater abilities contribute to her missions, and he gets to search for fellow Atlanteans.

In 1978, *Battlestar Galactica* debuted, and it, too, failed to make it to a second season. Its similarity to *Star Wars* helped generate lots of initial impact, but ultimately its special effects were *in*effective on the small screen, and lawsuits from 20th Century-Fox made more headlines than the individual episodes.

THE '80s AND '90s

V started out as a highly rated 10-hour miniseries in 1983, and went on the following year to become a less successful TV show that lasted for only one season. Earth is invaded by Nazi-like aliens that sometimes look

In this scene from *V*, Faye Grant is obviously having a bad day.

human but are really grotesque reptiles that eat rats and . . . humans. "*V*" refers to the resistance movement's symbol for victory. *V* creator Kenneth Johnson tried again in 1989 with *Alien Nation*, an L.A.–based cop show (based on the 1988 motion picture) in which one partner in a detective team is from the planet Tencton. He is one of a quarter million former Tenctonese slaves now stranded on Earth, trying to integrate for better or worse into our racist society. Its well-thought-out demonstrations of how the aliens are biologically and culturally different turn this would-be police drama into stylish science fiction. Despite cult followings, low ratings and high budgets killed *V* and *Alien Nation*.

 Quantum Leap, on the other hand, lasted for five seasons. Although it debuted in 1989, it will definitely be remembered as a top show of the '90s. Physicist Sam Beckett's Quantum Leap accelerator is a vehicle that enables him to time-travel and troubleshoot. He finds individuals in distress, "becomes them" for a time, and changes history for the better. TV viewers see Sam Beckett; those in Sam's presence see the person whose body he is inhabiting. He has assumed the bodies of, among others, an American Indian, Bobo the chimp, a contestant (female) in a beauty pageant and an exotic (male) dancer, someone with Down's syndrome, an FBI agent, a member of a motorcycle gang, a Ku Klux Klan member, a mother-to-be in labor, Lee Harvey Oswald, a priest, a rabbi, Dr. Ruth, a sexually harassed secretary and a date-rape victim, a superstar (male) rock singer and an aspiring (girl-group) lead vocalist, and his own self circa 1969. The possibilities for mixing hard drama with humor and bittersweet nostalgia were exploited to the max.

When *The X-Files* debuted in 1993, it quickly established itself as one of the best science fiction shows ever to grace the airwaves. It has won Golden Globe Awards for best drama, best actor (David Duchovny), and best actress (Gillian Anderson); in 1997, Anderson took home a best actress Emmy Award as well. Its premise is simple: Fox Mulder and Dana Scully are FBI agents who investigate unconventional crimes and paranormal activities.

Mulder realizes that traditional problem-solving skills don't always suffice; because he believes his little sister was long ago abducted by aliens, he has an open mind and pursues leads that his more limited peers would never follow. His nickname among the other agents is "Spooky."

His partner, Scully, on the other hand is a trained physician, a woman of science, a skeptic who tries to counter Mulder's fantastic imagination with plausible, provable explanations. But she also has the brains to not dismiss her brilliant partner's belief system.

The X-Files themselves are unsolved mysteries—

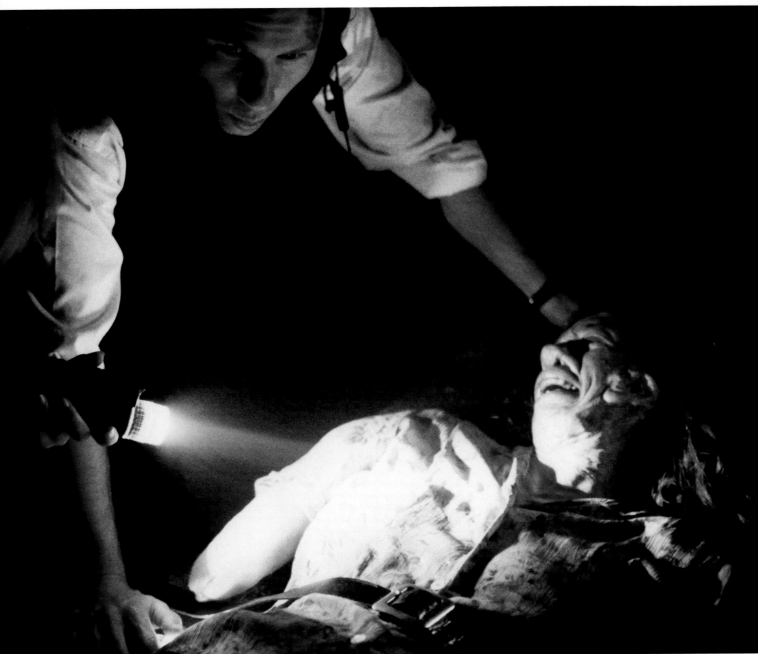

crimes that the FBI has never been able to fully explain. Mulder is thoroughly familiar with these cases and relies on them to solve present-day crimes. So, for instance, when a serial killer who steals the livers of his victims is at large, Scully presumes that it could not be the same man who has committed the exact same murders every 30 years since 1903. She's looking for a man in his 20s or 30s, not one in his 90s. Mulder, however,

knows the X-File and is certain the killer is one and the same. When they find a bile-filled nest, Mulder uncovers the truth: The killer is a mutant who eats fresh human livers and hibernates for 30 years, aging only a year between kills.

More than any other TV show in the genre, *The X-Files* is science fiction. Scully's character gives the show its scientific credibility; even if her theories are eventually disproved, science is her starting point. The show finds a way to do ghosts, vampires, UFOs, and faith healers—the stuff of great fantasy and horror adventures—without steering away from science.

The show's success can be largely attributed to a lack of trust in the government among the general populace that has escalated since the days of Watergate in the '70s and the Iran-Contra affair in the '80s. When *The X-Files* suggests a government cover-up about deadly viruses or contact with extraterrestrials, even the most patriotic '90s audience member has little trouble believing in such goings-on.

Its success is also due to its excellent story lines—even if they sometimes rely heavily on classic films for their inspiration. The Antarctica episode—in which scientists drill deep into the Earth and uncover a deadly creature who's been frozen since it crash-landed from outer space 20,000 years ago—is unabashedly derivative of *The Thing*. The artificial intelligence show in which a Central Operating System (COS) in a high-security skyscraper becomes murderous brings to mind HAL in *2001*. And Scully has on numerous occasions reminded us of another strong-yet-vulnerable female FBI agent: Clarice Starling in *The Silence of the Lambs*. But in those instances that the show does rely on previous works for its inspiration, it always does so with great taste and reverence.

Photo by Ruth Kyle

In an editorial in *Isaac Asimov's Science Fiction Magazine* (March–April 1978), Asimov wrote, "Science fiction is that branch of literature that deals with human responses to the changes in the level of science and technology." Now, if one were to attend a World Science Fiction Convention and ask 100 random participants to define the term *science fiction*, one would probably get as many different responses. Asimov's definition, therefore, is not necessarily the definitive one, but he pretty much earned the right to say whatever he wished (and change his mind!), and I for one think his statement is an excellent starting point. For it puts things into context: *Frankenstein* is science fiction because a doctor uses technological means to give life to the dead; *Dracula* is not. *Dracula* is great horror, feeding on our fear of things that only come out in the dark, but it has little to do with science.

That said, one must admit that some of the best stories mix the elements of science with horror or fantasy to produce something plausible. Taken in its post–World War I context, the film *Metropolis* is a warning about how technological improvements in the hands of a short-sighted tyrant could cause mass destruction. Orwell's novel *Nineteen Eighty-Four*, with its government-operated futuristic surveillance monitors watching one's every move, ages beautifully *well after* the year 1984 and will continue to be as chilling as it was upon its mid-century publication. And what makes *The X-Files* such effective television is that it persuades viewers to believe things they pray couldn't be true, such as deadly insect larvae germinating in pus-filled boils on human faces as by-products of government-sanctioned drug company research.

But science fiction need not be all Sturm und Drang. Like any genre, it has the right to be multi-faceted. Sci-fi can be light—the good-natured pranks of our favorite Martians and invisible men provide delightful entertainment. It can inspire wonder—as in the gorgeous urban landscape in *Just Imagine* and the sense of possibility in *E.T.* It can even be funny; just watch *Young Frankenstein.*

Alas, as we wind our way to the end of *Forrest J Ackerman's World of Science Fiction* and the end of the 20th century, it becomes apparent that there is less and less great new science fiction literature being written. The pulps during the Golden Age in the '30s and '40s provided a perfect venue for the relentless burst of creativity fueled by war, new technology, new industry. If there were 10 pulps on the stands in a given month with 10 stories inside—well, that's 100 stories a month right there, and Hollywood could never produce that (imagine 1,200 new scientifilms a year!). Nevertheless, by the 1950s, sci-fi was becoming Hollywood's property, and most of the great pulps are now long gone. Today, the most popular science fiction comes not from writers such as Kuttner and Moore, Russell, and Stapledon, but from filmmakers and directors and producers such as John Carpenter, George Lucas, and Steven Spielberg. Their talents are evident, their efforts are laudable, and they keep the genre thriving. But because I still adore the written word and because I know I don't have to persuade today's science fiction fans to see the latest *Star Trek* film (they already have, twice), I leave you with this thought: Go out and read the greats. Not just the Doyles and Wellses and Vernes, who are taught in school and already well-represented on film, but the lesser-knowns as well. The pulps may be collectors' items, but good paperback anthologies remain in print. Worlds of great imagination are waiting on bookstore shelves, anxious to jump out at you and cry, "You will *love* me!"

(Opposite) Hugo Gernsback, the Father of Science Fiction, and myself, the Son of Sci-Fi, at a convention in 1960. It was one of the thrills of my life to present Mr. Gernsback with his "Hugo" award.

FORRY RECOMMENDS

The three-volume *Encyclopedia of Science Fiction and Fantasy* compiled by Donald H. Tuck (1974, Advent:Publishers, Inc.) is "a bibliographic survey of the fields of science fiction, fantasy, and weird fiction through 1968." Unfortunately, it is probably only available in the reference section of some libraries at this point. It includes brief biographies and relatively complete bibliographies of all science fiction personalities, including those only published in the pulps. John Clute's *Science Fiction: The Illustrated Encyclopedia* (1995, Dorling Kindersley Limited) is both beautiful and scholarly, and is obviously more current. It includes authors, classic books, and films of the '70s, '80s, and '90s. Two other books were excellent sources of information about authors: E. F. Bleiler's *Science Fiction Writers* (1982, Charles Scribner's Sons) and Curtis Smith's *Twentieth-Century Science-Fiction Writers,* second edition (1986, St. James Press). Smith's volume is all-inclusive and thoughtful, but the entries are definitely encyclopedic in nature (with most subjects getting but a page or two), whereas

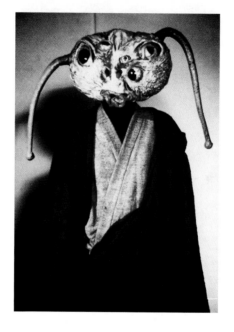

Bleiler's work presents lengthy critical essays about each author.

The Encyclopedia of Science Fiction Movies by Phil Hardy (1986, Octopus Books) is a comprehensive year-by-year presentation that covers 1895 through 1985. It offers critical analyses of each scientifilm; provides the major credits for each entry (directors, producers, screenwriters, cinematographers, special-effects wizards, and principal cast members); and lists all Academy Award nominees and winners. *The Film Encyclopedia* by Ephraim Katz (1990, Perennial Library), although not specific to science fiction, is another exhaustive collection that is filled with fabulous trivia.

As for television references, there are many, but *The Encyclopedia of TV Science Fiction* by Roger Fulton (1990, 1995, Boxtree Limited) is particularly useful to the sci-fi enthusiast. It contains an episode-by-episode presentation for each show, and includes cast members and writing credits, which is useful when you're trying to figure out which *Twilight Zone* featured Joan Blondell and which one was based on the Lewis Padgett (i.e., Kuttner and Moore) story.

GRATEFUL ACKNOWLEDGMENT IS EXPRESSED TO THE
FOLLOWING INDIVIDUALS, PUBLISHERS & MOTION
PICTURE STUDIOS FOR THE PARTS THEY
HAVE PLAYED IN THE CREATION OF THIS VOLUME

AIP, Air Wonder Stories, Brian W. Aldiss, J.C. Appelbaum, Arkham House, Isaac Asimov, Astonishing Stories, Astounding Stories, Neil Austin, Arthur Brooks Baker, Rick Baker, Harry Bates, Everett F. Bleiler, Hannes Bok, Ronald V. Borst, Anthony Boucher, Ray Bradbury, Bobbie Bresee, Kevin J. Burns, Edgar Rice Burroughs, H.J. Campbell, John W. Campbell, Mark Carducci, Ted Carnell, Dino Castrillo, Clayton Publishing, John Clute, Bill Crawford, Frank Darabont, Walter J. Daugherty, Marcel Delgado, Myrtle R. Douglas, Anton Drek, Edison Films, Elliott Dold Jr., Lloyd Arthur Eshbach, Experimenter Publishing Co., Famous Monsters of Filmland (Warren Publications), Fantasy Press, Fantasy Publishing Co. Inc., Virgil Finlay, Fleuve Noir, Brian Forbes, Georges Gallet, Stuart Gardner, Gaumont-British, Hugo Gernsback, Mary Gnaedinger, H.L. Gold, M. Gourday, Hadley Publishing, Jack Harris, Marilyn Harris, Ray Harryhausen, Robert A. Heinlein, Antonio Helu, Russell J. Hodgkins, Linus Hogenmiller, Charles D. Hornig, L. Ron Hubbard, Hugos, George Clayton Johnson, Alexander Korda, "Keep Watching the Skies!", Charles Keeping, Erle Korshak, Henry Kuttner, David A. Kyle, Carl Laemmle, John Landis, Fritz Lang, Verne Langdon, LASFS, Walt Lee, Murray Leinster, Los Cuentos Fantasticos, Robert A.W. Lowndes, Lucas Films, Bill Malone, Rouben Mamoulian, Ned Mann, Fredric March, Leo Margulies, Marvel Comics, Marvel Science Sories, A. Merritt, MGM, Bob Michelucci, Miracle Science & Fantasy Stories, Joe Moe, Mondadori Publishers, Morojo, Catherine L. Moore, Sam Moskowitz, Nebulas, National Portrait Gallery of London, Nebula Science Fiction, William F. Nolan. Willis O'Brien, Bob Olsen, Geo. Orwell, George Pal, Ray Palmer, Paramount, Frank R. Paul, Allan Rune Petersson, Jack Pierce, Tom & Terri Pinckard, Irwin Porges, Pyramid Books, Judson W. Reeves, Mark Reinsberg, Republic Pictures, RKO, Gene Roddenberry, Alva Rogers, Jean-Claude Romer, Theodore Roszak, Conrad H. Ruppert, Eric Frank Russell, Tom Savini, Ernest B. Schoedsack, Julius Schwartz, Science Fiction Digest, Science Fiction League, Science Wonder Stories, Rod Serling, Mary Shelley, Bob Short, Simon & Schuster, Clifford D. Simak, Curt Siodmak, Jack Speer, Startling Stories, Stirring Science Sories, A.W. Strickland, Super Science Stories, William F. Temple, Thrilling Wonder Stories, Tiffany, The Time Traveller, F. Orlin Tremaine, Twentieth Century Fox, UFA, Universal, A. Hyatt Verrill, A.E. van Vogt, Andy Warhol, Bill Warren, James Warren, Stanley G. Weinbaum, Mort Weisinger, H.G. Wells, Wesso, Olon F. Wiggins, Jack Willliamson, Donald A. Wollheim, Wordsworth Classics, Farnsworth Wright, S. Fowler Wright, Berni Wrightson, Belle Wyman, Geo. H. Wyman, Ziff-Davis Publishing Co.,